The Magician's
I Ching

The Magician's
I Ching

Swami Anand Nisarg

Aeon Books

First published 2015 by
Aeon Books
London NW3

Copyright © 2015 by Swami Anand Nisarg

British Library Cataloguing in Publication Data

A C.I.P. for this book is available from the British Library

ISBN-978-1-90465-865-8

Typeset by Alexandra Thornton, London

Printed in Great Britain

www.aeonbooks.co.uk

I declare my word: YI–FA, as the law of the universe

Table of Contents

Acknowledgements

Artistic Credit

Six-Dimensional Boolean Lattice Image artwork: Dr. Andreas Schöter (printed with permission).

Reprinted from www.yijing.co.uk.

Originally published in "The Yijing as a Symbolic Language for Abstraction", Proceedings of the 2nd International Conference on I-Ching (Yijing) Studies and Contemporary Civilization, 2005, pp. 291-305.

Nuclear Hexagram Image artwork: Ma Deva Kalika.

The "King Wen later heaven bagua" image (BenduKiwi) and "Tree of Life with Tarot attributions" image (by Alan SyncBook Press) are kindly reprinted from Wikipedia under its Creative Commons Attribution-Sharealike 3.0 Unreported license.

About the Author

Swami Anand Nisarg is a Tantrist Guru and teacher of the Mystery School, with a rebellious expectation-challenging style that has earned him the nickname of "the Anti-Swami". He has also been a student of the western esoteric tradition for over twenty years, and a practitioner of the I Ching for just as long (a period he barely considers enough to scratch the surface of its mysteries). An unexpected spiritual experience caused him to leave behind graduate-level university studies in Religious History in order to receive initiation under a Guru, and subsequent Enlightenment experiences led him to begin to offer initiation and teach techniques of Awareness to anyone who sought him out. Putting emphasis on the individual teacher-student relationship, and on making use of what works to unlock Awareness (be it western magick or eastern mysticism) his present school takes the form of dozens of dedicated initiates, hundreds who have participated in his workshops and online programs, and many thousands who have watched his YouTube lecture series. In addition to this book, he is the author of "Three Paths of Ecstasy" (a guide to mysticism), "Song of the Blessed One" (a translation and commentary on the Bhagavad Gita), and several online books (most freely available, some reserved for students of his Intensive Mysticism Program one-on-one program; or the "Magick for Mystics" or "Tantra for Transcending" courses).

Preface

This work is not an academic work. It is not the product of a professional sinologist. Those who are engaged with serious Chinese historical study or have studied the historical context of the I Ching will no doubt find that while this book delves far more into the Chinese context of the I Ching than many others on the popular market, there will be a number of things missing from what would constitute a properly "academic" work. Likewise, they may find that some of the concepts and choices in the material seem unusual, that certain things may seem presented or emphasized in ways that do not fit the traditions, that some of the work appears radical, if not to say "wrong".

In order to clarify: this book is written from the point of view of a mystic and magician. While what meagre training I have as an historian has been put to some use in the development of this book, its central source is the hidden wisdom that is revealed through actual practice and intense experimentation with the material. The first priority in the writing of The Magician's I Ching is to create a book that will be of great practical utility to the western practitioner of the I Ching, whether novice or already experienced. The historical information in this book is slanted toward the promotion of the teaching of universal mysticism. The I Ching's text is not intended to be a literal translation but rather an interpretation based on decades of esoteric practice with both the I Ching and mysticism in general (in both eastern and western traditions). It is an interpretation, with the goal of demonstrating how the I Ching can be used authentically but with ease by western practitioners (and any eastern practitioners interested in the western perspective). First and foremost, it is a text to be used, not treated as an academic work for study or the affirmation of academic theories.

It is my hope that academics and non-academics alike will be able to find the perspective of this book refreshing and useful, and that it will not only make them think about the I Ching, but also encourage them to engage in practice (or in deeper practice) with it; possibly incorporating it further into their overall agenda of spiritual/esoteric exercises. However, if there are any who read this book and take offence to its approach, or wish to get stuck in righteous indignation of its no-doubt significant gaps of historical exposition or lack of academic rigour, I will quote the Great Beast in his suggestion that such people are free to "absorb their Yang into their own Yin, as the Americans say". Whatever modern academia may have concluded rightly or wrongly about the I Ching, this book represents what I have concluded about it, thus far.

The Unfolding of the Changes

In the beginning, there is nothing.

Nothing creates Nothingness.

Nothingness creates a Nothingness impregnated with potential.

This Pregnant Nothingness gives birth to All.

The All divides itself into the One and the Two.

These give way to Enlightenment.

Enlightenment expands into the Sun, Fire, Water, Air, Earth, and the Moon.

These various elements contract into The World.

Swami Anand Nisarg

Note I

If You Are An Absolute Beginner at I Ching

If you have no familiarity with the I Ching at all before reading this book, don't despair! You will find everything you need to work with the I Ching here. This is not just a beginner's book, however, so you shouldn't try to do everything at once or allow yourself to be overwhelmed by all the material here.

I would suggest that you start by reading the introduction. You may wish to quickly review Chapter One (though you will likely find some of its concepts to be quite heavy; do not worry if you do not understand all of them yet; re-reading this chapter once you have learned the basics of the I Ching system will be more fruitful). Read Chapter Two to learn how to perform I Ching castings, and then review the main text of the I Ching (Chapter Three). Then even before looking into the rest of the material, start trying to work with the I Ching. Try out the divination system, see what it does for you. As you work, then you can keep reading the rest of the book and taking a closer look at the rest of the material at your own pace. You will find that the I Ching (and the material in this book) is not just something that's read in a single sitting and then put aside; it is something to look over repeatedly, while you actually work on it. Don't get frustrated if there are parts that seem incomprehensible at first; the main thing is to keep practising with the I Ching; and as you go along you'll develop your own insights. Then, as you keep reviewing the instructional material, this will open up new ideas and perspectives, which will in turn strengthen your practice. At this time you will want to try to adopt some of the guidelines in Appendix I as to how to methodically study the I Ching. In this way you'll develop into a practitioner of the Yi-Fa. The I Ching rewards those who learn by practicing.

Note II

If You Are A Western Magician

You don't have to be a practitioner of Magick to make use of this version of the I Ching; the material is set up so that it is self-contained, so that it can enhance a magical practice. However such a practice is not a requirement for the book's use.

If you are a western magician, and are new to working with the I Ching, I would suggest you follow the same guidelines as in "note 1" above. If, however, you are quite familiar with magical theory, you will likely find Chapter One (and the section on correspondences in Chapter Four) more enlightening than a raw beginner would.

The I Ching has a long tradition in western magical practice, beginning with Aleister Crowley who used it for decades as his primary method of divination. Its practice increased in popularity in the 1960s; and while some modern authors have included material on the I Ching in books on western magick, I believe this is the first attempt at creating a version of the I Ching that is specifically meant to lend itself to the western esoteric practitioner. In addition to the main text being specifically organized and worded to focus on utility for practice, for being used in actual divination, I have structured the philosophy of the I Ching in such a way as to make clear its parallels to concepts in western Magick. In particular, the ideas about the "Superior Individual" have strong parallels with the Thelemic teachings on True Will, and the concept of the Yi-Fa is here treated as a magical word and current. I have also chosen to place in a primary position those elemental titles for the eight trigrams that most easily correspond to the western elemental system (and in the main text, I refer to them by their elemental names, rather than their Chinese names).

I trust that whether you have already ventured into the I Ching, or are starting on it now to complement your other magical studies, you will find this edition particularly useful to adding new tools to your magical arsenal in the performance of the Great Work.

Introduction

In one of the Commentaries on the I Ching, the great Chinese scholar Confucius, master of the I Ching, was asked "Can the thoughts of the great ancient sages not be recorded in full?" He answered: "Writing cannot contain such profound insights in full; language cannot communicate it in full. But this is why the sages created Symbols to express their concepts in full: the sixty-four hexagrams (of the I Ching) are made to represent all the true and false states of Reality in full, the oracles and line descriptions of the same express what the Sages wished to explain in full; and the lines (of the I Ching) can change to their opposite to benefit all people, so that anyone can come to understand Reality".

The I Ching is an ancient and profound system of divination comparable to the Tarot or the Runes; and like these, it is much more than the simple fortune-telling device that most use it for today. Its success is indicated by the fact that it is one of the most ancient sacred texts to continue in uninterrupted use to this day; it is at least 3,000 years old.

It is, in its essence, a system of classification for self-analysis, that allows its student to obtain a greater understanding of the nature of external reality and his interior self. When adequately studied, the I Ching allows one to engage in deep contemplation and to receive practical advice to the challenges of the moment.

In spite of this, there are certain challenges faced by the student of the I Ching, particularly the western student; whether he is a beginner, someone versed in western esoteric practices, or someone who has attempted to study eastern mysticism. Issues of time, distance, and translation have all acted as barriers to many would-be students of this worthwhile system.

The I Ching is in fact the oldest known occult teaching in continual common usage in human history; in its most primitive forms it may have been used as long as 5,000 years ago. The Tarot, by contrast, is only about 500 years old. The I Ching book itself is the world's oldest book still in common use. Scholars generally agree that the oracle system has existed in written form since 1100 BCE, though some theories suggest that earlier written copies could have been even older in more prototypical forms, as other manuals for the same system of divination as the I Ching. The surviving version, which we use to this day, was the manual devised by the Zhou, but some records of Chinese history suggest that at one point this was only one of various manuals, created in different regions for this divination system .

The system of the I Ching contains within it complex mathematical concepts: the I Ching system is the oldest known example of a binary code (4,500 years before Liebnitz, who found himself stunned when a Jesuit missionary priest showed him a translation of the I Ching, and he realized the Chinese had developed binary code thousands of years earlier). Its sixty four different hexagrams can be combined into different logical progressions that contain surprisingly sophisticated mathematical ideas: besides the binary, it was only recently discovered that the standard format of the 64-hexagram sequence (the "King Wen" sequence) in fact expresses a projection of a "six-dimensional hyper-lattice". In terms of what it says about the nature of change, the implications of the I Ching has fascinated scholars in the West since its introduction. One group of particular note that was heavily influenced by the I Ching and its philosophy were the early quantum physicists: Neils Bohr, Werner Heisenberg, and Erwin Schrodinger were all students of the I Ching. It was so influential on Bohr that when he was granted a coat of arms by his grateful government he placed the Tao at its centre.

The original eight elemental trigrams from which the entire I Ching system is derived were said by Chinese tradition to have been discovered on the back of a turtle shell by the (mythological) Chinese emperor Fu Xi (who would have ruled sometime around 3100bce). Fu Xi was also said in varied legendary accounts to have invented writing, fishing and marriage. According to traditional historical accounts, it was another (this time definitively non-mythological) monarch, King Wen of Zhou, who first provided the detailed explanation of the hexagrams that became the core text of the I Ching (thus, the core of the I Ching is called the "Zhou Yi"). The title of "king" was posthumously given to Wen by his son, who became the first true King of Zhou; in his own time Wen was a vassal ruler of the Zhou province of the mighty (but decadent) Shang Kingdom. The Shang were so concerned with the possibility of Wen leading the Zhou into open rebellion that they

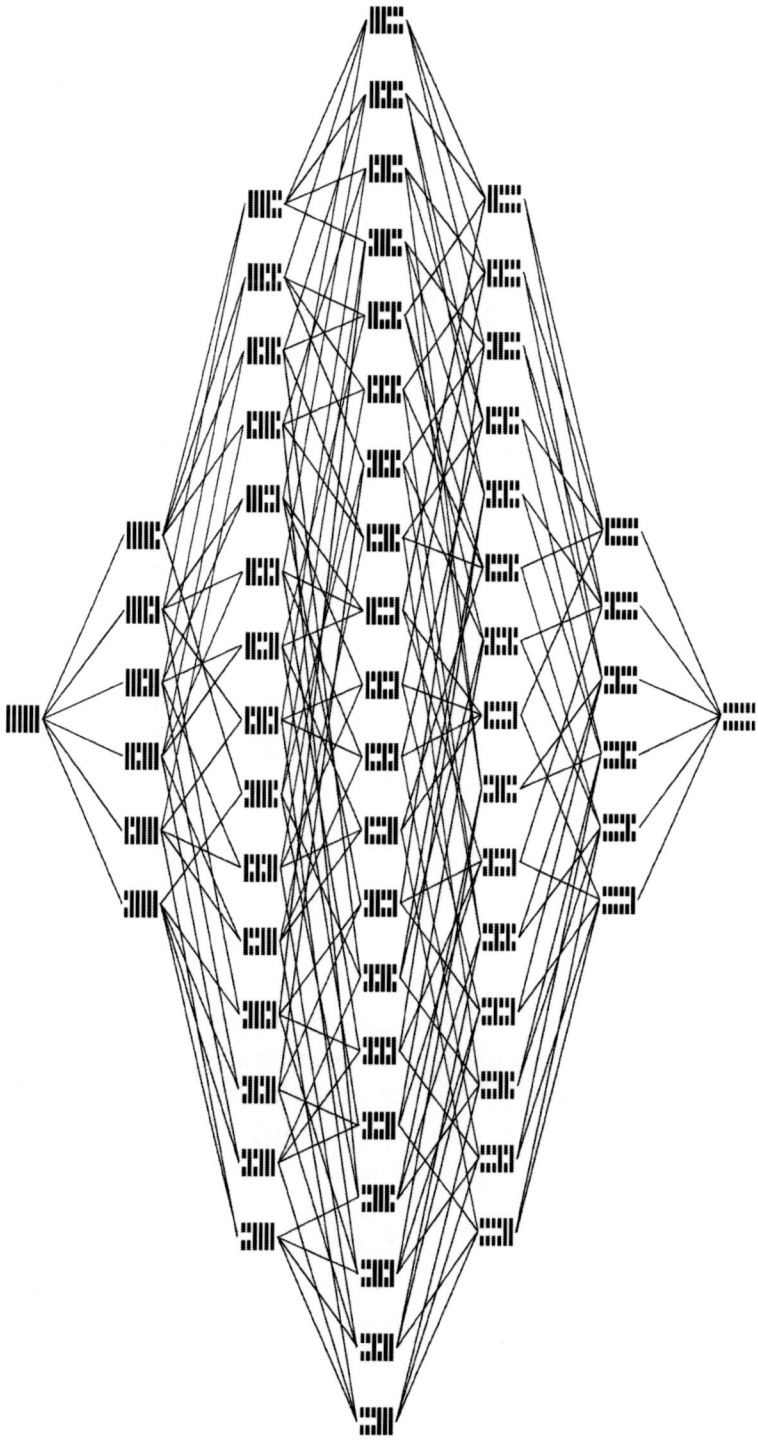

Six-Dimensional Boolean Lattice of Hexagrams; http://www.yijing.co.uk

imprisoned him; and legend holds that Wen wrote the I Ching while he was jailed. After his death, his sons led the rebellion and overthrew the Shang, whose kingdom collapsed, and the Zhou grew to become the dominant kingdom of ancient China at that time. One of King Wen's sons, the Duke of Zhou, was also credited with completing his father's work on the I Ching.

The rest of the I Ching, here termed the "Commentaries", is attributed to Confucius. However, from a point of view of academic history, it seems highly likely that the Commentaries were not written by Confucius as such, but rather collected (again probably posthumously) by his students. This does not necessarily imply some kind of falsification; the Commentaries were certainly written by Confucians, and likely contained in them accounts of his teachings on the I Ching over many years and different occasions. In either case, there's no question that Confucius was a great admirer of the I Ching and declared it one of the "Five Classics" of Chinese knowledge; Confucius was said to have once said as an old man "If I could live just a few more years, I would have dedicated sixty of them to the study of the I Ching". After Confucius' time, the I Ching became a central part of the mainstream Chinese intellectual and spiritual world (unlike the Tarot, which is unfortunately relegated to the fringes of our culture); it continued to be studied by the brightest thinkers and deepest mystics of Chinese history, and many of these provided new concepts and innovations, which added to the I Ching system.

One significant challenge with the I Ching from a western perspective is the straightforward issue of translations. There are a great many translations of the I Ching, and while many are quite good, some have of course been better or more notable than others. Of particular note in the early period of the I Ching's popularization in the West are the translations by Legge (published in 1882, and deeply flawed due to issues with correct translations of the time), one of the earliest for public consumption; Wilhelm (published in German in 1923, translated to English in 1951, which suffered from being a translation of a translation and being excessively academic); Aleister Crowley (not published in his lifetime, suffering from translation issues due to the limitations of his time, and remade in a poetic format not original to the I Ching), and Blofeld (1965, perhaps the best early mystical translation though still lacking in sufficient practical context). In recent years there has been a plethora of new translations, some of which benefited from more accurate attention to the original text, while others were less regular interpretations that incorporated new age thought, significantly re-wrote the text, or fused the I Ching with particular thematic agendas.

In general, these and other translations tend to have one of two problems: either they have a serious academic focus, leading to versions that put more emphasis on literal translation and on providing the full Confucian commentaries (which can be very rewarding to read but can also be intimidating to the beginner and are not designed to be practical for actual use), or they tend to be watered-down or diluted versions of the I Ching with the addition of concepts from pop-psychology or new-age thinking, perhaps "made simple", but not made more useful for it.

Many of the more literal or scholarly translations will tend to corral the mind into one particular direction of understanding the written verses, sometimes causing the would-be I Ching user to avoid opening up his awareness to receive a more intuitive application of his reading to his own use. If one gets too caught up in intellectual analysis of a line of the I Ching, it reduces the likelihood that comes from being open to understanding its possible implications, in a way more open to one's own situation, in the context of the moment of the reading. On the other hand, a translation that fails to maintain sufficient accuracy to transmit the underlying philosophical and esoteric concepts will make it difficult for deeper spiritual reception to occur, and risks reducing the I Ching to the status of a common oracle.

Many lines in the I Ching are unintentionally rendered more obscure or incomprehensible than they should be, due to a sometimes too-literal translation of the text. While there are several truly good literal and technical translations of the I Ching, there are few if any that do a good job of what could be called the "symbolic translation". Likewise, many attempts at "simplifying" or "westernizing" the I Ching lose all of the sophistication of the system, and reduce the hexagrams and lines to one-dimensional oracles of little more worth than a fortune cookie.

The symbolism of the I Ching is a language that is sometimes foreign to the western experience. While symbols in terms of esoteric understanding are universal, coming all from the common source of the human experience, the way different cultures express and order these symbols are variable, and this can create difficulties in comprehension. On the most superficial level of this phenomenon, there are a number of verses in the literal translation of the I Ching that are in fact figures of speech, common and understandable to someone familiar with Chinese culture at the time they were recorded (and some of which have gone on to become modern aphorisms), but that would not automatically be understandable to someone who is not.

At a more fundamental level, the usual translations of the most basic elemental symbolism of the I Ching are framed in the historical "ordering" of the elements in Chinese mysticism; which are not quite the same as those of western mysticism. This is not to say that both cultures use different symbols, rather it is that the way they express this symbolism is different; and if you translate these expressions literally, you end up confusing the clarity of the symbolic intention or ordering of the elements. To give one particularly egregious example, the trigrams Chien (☰) and Kun (☷), which are the basic positive/ negative trigrams, are usually translated as "Heaven" and "Earth" respectively. Now, "heaven" is not a poor choice of word for the Chien trigram (you could use "celestial", or "sky", or even "phallus" in its function as the symbolic masculine). The use of "Earth" for Kun, on the other hand, creates a number of problems; thinking about it makes it clear that the "Earth" referred to is "the world" (juxtaposed with Chien's "heaven"), but using the word "earth" confuses this trigram with the concept of the "Earth Element", one of the four basic elements. Complicating matters further, the four elements are a part of the trigrams as well, and the trigram that would represent the "Earth Element", Ken (☶) is usually translated as "Mountain". A student of western mysticism who is familiar with western alchemy, astrology, the Tarot, the Qabalah or other western systems of metaphysics might not realize that the trigram for "Mountain" is supposed to represent the same symbolic concept as the "Earth element"; as found in the hermetic earth element, the Taurus sign, the suit of coins, etc. The situation becomes much simpler for western practitioners if they come to understand the eight trigrams as representing the four elements in two sets: the four basic elements (Earth, Air, Water, Fire) in their "terrestrial" form, and their equivalent in the "celestial" form (as Moon, Sun, The World, and Heaven).

This version of the I Ching is not meant to be a new literal translation; rather, it is a re-writing of the I Ching, based on the goal of creating a version of that sacred book that focuses on the fundamental core of the I Ching text, with all details and commentaries presented in such a way as to assist in the application of the I Ching as a mystical and divination text. Likewise, it will remain true to the essential spirit of the "system for organizing reality" that the I Ching expresses, but will present the text and components of the I Ching in a way that is more directly related to the language in which western mysticism expresses these symbols. A sincere effort has been made to keep only the most essential expression of each line of the text, never adding any material that isn't absolutely necessary for understanding, but when possible rephrasing verses that make reference to "figures of speech" into plain English. In this way, it is my hope that this version of the I Ching will be ideal for use to the actual practitioner (particularly westerners who may be engaged in a western magical or mystical tradition), and to the individuals who actually want to use the I Ching for contemplation and self-enquiry (as part of the process western esotericism calls "The Great Work"), as well as divination practice.

Chapter One

The Esoteric Foundations of the I Ching

Tao, Yin, and Yang

To start with, understand that the I Ching is a model of reality, of space and time.

So imagine that out of the primordial nothingness there comes a "something".

That "something" is the Tao.

The Tao is oneness, it is completely alone, and thus cannot comprehend itself.

So it separates into two parts which are contained within it; thus from nothing, to oneness, you now have "twoness" (duality): Yang and Yin.

So first there is a complete oneness that can't really be comprehended intellectually at all; but within it, there are two basic and "opposite" forces: a strong and weak force, or positive and negative, or masculine and feminine.

Those are Yang and Yin.

These, in turn, continue to break down into more complex forms, representing the right elements (the four higher or "celestial" elements, and the four worldly or "terrestrial" elements).

You can think of these as the building blocks of the universe.

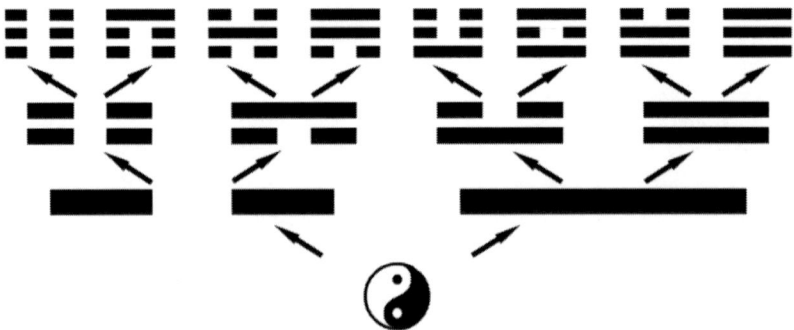

These sets of elements combine with each other, forming the sixty-four Hexagrams; which are combinations of two elements each (including those hexagrams that consist of two of the same element). Now, how do these elements form and reform? Through the process of time: as time goes by, strong forces break down into weak forces and weak forces build up into strong forces.

So the I Ching teaches the nature of time/change, and also allows us, inasmuch as we study and understand it, to predict the patterns of how changes happen over time.

The structure for understanding the I Ching begins with the Tao. The Tao is the term for the pure force of the universe. It is whole, eternal, and ineffable. It is said in the Tao Te Ching, the great teaching on the subject written by the master Lao Tzu, that "whatever can be described is not the Tao".

The basic way to conceive of the Tao is to think of it as the concept of zero. It is emptiness, but also eternity.

The Tao itself can be seen at a variety of levels: as pure emptiness, as an emptiness that has a quality of emptiness, as an emptiness that has the quality of fullness (that is, an emptiness that is "pregnant with potential"), or as a vast fullness.

At that final level of understanding, of a vast fullness, one can at first understand this Tao as a completely undefined fullness, just full with a pure energy.

Beyond that, one can understand this "full Tao" as containing within it the forces of all opposites; that is the Tao as the "union of opposites".

It is from this Tao that actual opposites emerge, emanating from the will to express emptiness as form; and at their most basic, they are the positive and negative, the yes and the no, the black and white, light and dark, male and female, up and down, strong and weak, creative and receptive. In other words, they are the primordial opposites.

In the metaphysics of the I Ching, the term for these two forces are "Yang" and "Yin". The "Yang" is the basic positive force. It is represented in the I Ching by a single straight unbroken line; thus, it is the "one".

The "Yin" is the basic negative force. It is represented in the I Ching by a single line broken into two parts by a gap, space, or void in the middle; thus, it is the "two".

It is these lines, the solid Yang and broken Yin lines, that make up all the trigrams of the I Ching.

The Trigrams

"Trigram" is the basic term for the symbols that represent the disparate elements that form the building blocks of the universe (as organized in the I Ching). They are called "trigrams" because they consist of three lines, each line being either a "Yin" or "Yang".

As the Yang is "one", and Yin is "two", the subsequent elements that are composed of combinations of these must have three parts. This is because two lines of pure Yin would just be Yin extended, two lines of pure Yang would just be Yang extended, and the two lines composed of Yin and Yang would be just "Yin and Yang", annihilating each other but not really adding anything new. Thus, the two-line combinations of Yin and Yang are only intermediate states; by definition they must proceed to a further state, which creates something truly new and stable. In order for there to be something truly new that is born of the mixture of Yin and Yang, it is necessary for there to be a synthesis, a mix of three parts, that (excepting the two extremes of three pure Yin lines or three pure Yang lines) consist of an unequal mixture of the two forces. Every mixed trigram will have either more Yin or more Yang, representing this mixture. Likewise, the presence of three lines means that the location of the Yin or Yang lines (which is on top, which is on the bottom, and which is in the middle) becomes important and creates difference between the forms.

The end result is the creation of eight trigrams, which represent eight fundamental forces in the alchemical universe of the I Ching. They are as follows:

☰ "Chien": Heaven

Chien is the trigram traditionally translated as "Heaven". It is pure Yang, solid and unbroken. It is the celestial power, all the energy of creating, strong, the cold force, the masculine, the phallus, light, the father. It is the quality of forcefulness. Its key spiritual concept is "Creative".

☷ "Kun": The World

Kun is the trigram traditionally translated as "earth", but its meaning is "The World" (the opposite of Chien, which is "Heaven"). Kun is pure Yin, broken lines. It is the worldly power, all the content of creation, weak, the hot force, the feminine, the yoni, darkness, the mother. It is the quality of spaciousness; as Heaven is the "force", so is World the "field". Its key spiritual concept is "Receptive".

☲ "Li": The Sun

Li has traditionally been translated as "fire", but this is the concept of pure primordial fire, not the lesser elemental fire. Thus, the best translation for this trigram is another historical attribution, which would put it in line with what "Li" is meant to represent in western esotericism: "The Sun". It is sometimes also referred to as "lightning". It is the trigram associated with summer (when the sun is at its strongest), beauty, and the power of clinging. Because it is a single weak line between two strong ones, it is referred to as the "middle daughter". Its quality is radiance. Its key spiritual concept is "Elegance".

☵ "Kan": The Moon

Kan has been traditionally translated as "water", but in the same way that Li represents primordial fire, Kan represents primordial water, thus another traditional attribution is a more appropriate one for western correspondence: "The Moon". It is also referred to sometimes as the cloud, or the pit. It can represent "danger", because of its hidden power (a strong line surrounded by weak lines). It is associated with winter (when the sun is at its weakest), the characteristic of enveloping; and because of the strong line in the middle it is called the "middle son". Its quality is depth. Its key spiritual concept is "Abysmal" (i.e., "Deep").

☳ "Chen": The Fire Element

The trigram "Chen" is traditionally translated as "thunder", but its quality is that of the hermetic element of Fire. It is the active and moving force, the force of dynamic power, the arousing or energetic force.It is correspondent to springtime, the time of rising force. Because of its single strong line at the bottom (the first line of the trigram, because in the I Ching the lines are always read from the bottom to the top), it is called the "eldest son". Its quality is vibration. Its key spiritual concept is "Arousing" (i.e., "Exciting").

☰ "Tui": The Water Element

The trigram "Tui" is traditionally translated as "lake", but its quality is that of the hermetic element of Water. It is the deep and still force. It corresponds to autumn, when nature is slowing down. It is also sometimes translated as "a marsh", or even a "swamp" (but this is somewhat inaccurate, as it is not meant to have any of the negative connotations westerners associate with swamps). It has the quality of the rain, of joy and relaxed pleasure. Because of its broken line at the top, it is called the "youngest daughter". Its quality is openness. Its key spiritual concept is "Pleasant" (or "Complacent").

☴ "Sun": The Air Element

The trigram "Sun" is traditionally translated as "wind", but its quality is that of the hermetic element of Air, which is also part of its traditional attributions. It is sometimes also translated as "wood", which is correspondent in Taoist alchemy to some of the concepts of the Air element, and like the hermetic air element corresponds to the intellect. It has a gentle but insistent quality. Because of its weak line at the bottom, it is called the "eldest daughter". Its quality is consideration. Its key spiritual concept is "Flexible".

☶ "Ken": The Earth Element

The trigram "Ken" is traditionally translated as "mountain", but its quality is that of the hermetic element of Earth, which attribution is clearly included in its traditional symbolism. It is the immovable solid power, and has the quality of stubbornness and stuckness. Because of its strong line at the top, it is called the "youngest son". Its quality is attachment. Its key spiritual concept is "Solid".

Thus it can be understood that the unfolding of the trigrams follows logical patterns, which are worthy of countless hours of contemplation, and have important similarities to systems found in the West (such as the Qabalah). The zero of the Tao becomes the one and two of the Yang and Yin lines; these lines in their purest form express as the forces of Heaven and The World (the creative power and the creation). Mingling, these forces become the Sun and the Moon (the balance of the weak in the strong, and the balance of the strong in the weak). Then they express themselves as the four elements, representing less balanced mixtures of weak and strong forces. Fire is the "eldest son", a strong base with weak middle and top. Water is the "eldest daughter", a weak top with a strong base and middle. Air is the "youngest daughter", a weak bottom with a strong middle and top; and Earth is the "youngest son", a strong top with a weak base and middle.

These eight forces, the trigrams, combine with each other, mingling to form sixty four different combinations (hexagrams) representing different states. Here is where the expression of the I Ching reaches its peak and most practical function: it describes any situation or state of the moment as a combination of two main influences, one below and the other above, interacting with one another to create the particular conditions in a person's life.

The I Ching, Taoism, and Confucian Thought (or True Will and the Great Work)

In western esotericism there is a term: "The Great Work". It refers to the overall goals of the practitioner. These goals are no less than to rectify the universe, to restore harmony between opposing forces by uniting them, and in that way reaching to the absolute. On a more practical level, the "Great Work" can be understood to be what in Sanskrit is called "Sādhāna", your entire spiritual discipline. It is everything you do to lead to that ultimate transformation; first of your own being, and then of the Universe itself. As I will elaborate in the following sections, there is a clear parallel to this teaching found in the philosophy and structure of the I Ching, and thus the I Ching can be invaluable both as a guide and an aid to accomplishing the Great Work.

Transformation Through Symbols (Taoist Study of Nature)

In the West, there are certain schools of esoteric practice that could be considered to be falling under the umbrella term of "magick". Far from involving the mere casting of spells or curses as is popularly imagined, magick (written with a "k" to distinguish it from the stagecraft of "magic tricks" and illusions) is primarily concerned with the same ideas of transformation and divine union as the often equally misrepresented and maligned eastern traditions like Tantra or Taoist Alchemy; indeed magick can be considered the western parallel to these esoteric traditions. In western magick, students are advised to direct their attention to divination as a subject of lifelong study; this being one of the earliest steps in their occult training. In part, this is because divination both requires and develops the understanding of the self in order to work, and understanding the self is a crucial stage in being able to transcend the self.

But more importantly, it is because any divination system that actually works must of necessity involve the interaction on an experiential (and not just intellectual) level with primordial symbols. And there is no better tool than an actual interactive practice by which to learn the "language" of symbols; it allows one to understand the nature and qualities of those primordial forces that will need to be effectively manipulated (at subsequent stages of training) to create change in accordance with one's true Will. For example, in a western esoteric school, students might be encouraged from the very earliest stages of training to familiarize themselves with the Tarot in order to both better understand their own subconscious, and to be exposed in an interactive and organic way to the constituent symbols and concepts of the Qabalistic Tree of Life. In this way, they will be able to refer to the rich tapestry of Tarot imagery when subsequently learning the structure of the Hermetic Qabalah. Diligent students who experience interacting with the Tarot cards and relating their readings to elements of their own life will later on find it much easier to learn how to likewise interact with those primordial forces (the elements, the planets, etc.) that are found on the Tree of Life, and create a similar "'magical link" when trying to tap into these forces in rituals of invocation for the purpose of transforming one's life or creating radical shifts in one's perspective.

So when we are studying symbols we are really meant to be studying reality. Now, the symbol is not in itself the "thing": the Taoists made this plain in their saying "the Tao which can be described is not the Tao". This is like saying that the word "fire", or the letters F-I-R-E, do not in themselves constitute a real fire. So great caution must be taken to avoid confusing the symbolic language, which is a kind of filing system for reality, for reality itself. At the same time, the Tao teaches that the "symbol" also cannot be truly divorced from the "thing" itself. What is above is like that which is below. The word "fire" is not in and of itself a fire, but it is also inextricably connected in our consciousness to capital-f Fire as a concept; it is a part of fire, it has a correspondence to it, though it is not the thing itself.

Thus, to study the I Ching correctly we must also study nature; which is to say everything in the ordinary reality that surrounds us. At the same time we must understand correspondence; observing nature, we can uncover secrets through symbols, like the legendary King Fu Xi did.

Fu Xi

In I Ching legend, before Confucius or the later philosophers, before King Wen, there was King Fu Xi. Unlike those other figures, everything we know about Fu Xi comes from ancient myth, and it is even possible that no such person ever actually existed.

According to some legends, Fu Xi and his sister were the last survivors of the human race after a great flood swept the earth. They survived by going to Kunlun Mountain, the great mountain at the centre of the world (the Chinese version of the "Holy Mountain" that exists as a symbol in most cultures). The previous civilization, a matriarchal culture that existed in a primitive state, was completely destroyed. The Celestial Emperor bade Fu Xi and his sister to wed and they produced the new human race, which was patriarchal, and began to develop civilization.

In this sense, the legend of Fu Xi is both the Chinese version of the archetypal flood-myth and of the story of the "Culture Hero", the equivalent of Prometheus, who brings humanity out of an animal-like state and starts the path to civilization. Before Fu Xi, human beings ate meat raw; he taught them how to cook with fire. He taught them how to fish with nets and lay traps, and how to forge hunting weapons. He taught them how to make musical instruments. He showed them the secret of the Word, and of how to record language. It is said he even uncovered the most fundamental biological and occult truth of humanity: before Fu Xi, people believed that babies were produced spontaneously in a woman's womb. It was Fu Xi who revealed that the male was required to inseminate a woman in order to produce offspring.

It is notable that although Fu Xi has miraculous powers in many of the stories about him, he is a human being. He also discovers civilization not through the Gods (although certainly supernatural elements are involved) but via the study of natural phenomena. While he is attributed with having made a number of specific inventions and discoveries (including the institution of marriage!) his greatest teaching is the power of observation, of learning (and potentially learning anything) by careful study of nature and the cycles of the world. In magical terms, Fu Xi represents the transition between what is sometimes referred to as the "Aeon of Isis" into the "Aeon of Osiris"; from the state of humanity-as-infants, acting through instinct and feeling alone, to the state of humanity-as-thinkers, able to build up civilizations by "obedience to the will of heaven" and observing and interacting with their environment.

(We are now at the start of a new aeon, the "Aeon of Horus", where we are discovering how to create our own environment, rather than being helpless to it, or having to work within its limits.)

The discovery of the trigrams of the I Ching is universally considered Fu Xi's greatest and most fundamental revelation; because it was through the understanding of the Trigrams, the symbolic building-blocks and the programming language of the universe, that Fu Xi was able to understand the nature around him and make all of his other innovations.

According to legend, Fu Xi first saw the trigrams of the I Ching on the shell of a turtle that emerged from the Luo River; as in other cultures, the great rivers of China were considered sacred (goddesses in themselves, much like the Ganges and other Indian rivers are goddesses), and so this story can be understood to represent the emergence of Symbol from the primordial Divine Feminine. Indeed, in Taoist mysticism this river is associated with the cosmos, so the emergence of the turtle from the river is equivalent to the reception of these symbols from the universe itself. It was the "birth" of Symbol, of the Word from deep silence, of structure from flowing chaos. Deciphering these symbols (which were also mathematics, the mysteries of number, and geometry), Fu Xi then dedicated himself to look for their qualities in nature, and discovered that by applying them to nature, he could see how to work with nature to create change. In other words, Fu Xi was the first true Chinese practitioner of high Magick. If Magick is understood as the "art or science of causing change to occur in conformity to the Will" (Aleister Crowley's definition), then it was through the "magick" of the eight trigrams that Fu Xi understood that by applying fire to meat you could prepare food; and that when masculine and feminine converge in intercourse they produce offspring (thus allowing not only the creation of social institutions but also the raising of livestock).

Today, the I Ching invites us to do the same. And just as all of Fu Xi's discoveries have a symbolic esoteric significance, so too can we apply the study of the I Ching to giving us tools to observe, understand, and adapt to reality (or indeed, adapt reality, by predicting the flow of change over time) in our material world; and likewise to achieve breakthroughs in comprehending those other dimensions of reality that exist within our consciousness, learning how to manipulate the inner elements (terrestrial and celestial) within our own nature in order to harmonize and transform ourselves.

Confucius: Seeking the Superior Individual (Philosophy of the Will)

While Taoism, or perhaps the even older tradition of "Wu" witchcraft that preceded it, was the foundational source of the I Ching, the I Ching as it exists today is impregnated with Confucian philosophy. This is largely to its benefit, as the development of Confucian thought transforms the already valuable divinatory tool and mystical text into a fully realized guide to self-transformation.

If you were to remove the Confucian philosophy from the I Ching, you would still have a text of significant mystical and symbolic worth, far more than most mere "fortune-telling" types of oracles. However, the mysticism of the core-text I Ching (the oldest part of the book, called the Zhou Yi) would amount to a guide to right action in accord with nature; how to react to situations and adapt to them. It is the Confucian philosophy that adds to it the element of profound instruction in personal alchemy.

In the West, Confucianism has been largely ignored in comparison to other eastern religions that have become highly popular (perhaps because of how wrapped up Confucianism is with Chinese culture). Taoism, largely misinterpreted as a lackadaisical "do whatever you feel like" hippie-religion, has become quite popular; while Confucianism is erroneously thought of as a stuffy system dedicated largely to government bureaucracy and social control. This is in fact a serious misinterpretation; however it is understandable why people might think that way. The popular image many in the West have of Confucianism is actually closer to the philosophy known as "Legalism", which was an ideology strictly interested in the structuring of a stable society. In fact, Confucianism was a historical opponent of legalism (and the Legalists at one point attempted to persecute and destroy Confucianism, making it a capital offence during the Qin dynasty). However, over time much of Legalism's mentality has crept into mainstream Confucianism, and late/modern Confucianism is fairly stiff, its original mystical underpinnings having had few advocates as it became more materialistic in response to the mystical elements of its chief competitors: Taoism and Buddhism.

Nevertheless, the Confucianism of ancient China, over the course of more than a millennium, was profound; producing some truly astounding mystical thinkers and dedicated to no less than seeking to comprehend the Universe and one's place in it. Yet it was dedicated not only to adapting to the ways of nature, but also to the transformation of the individual.

The Confucian commentaries of the I Ching add a vital element to its structure: the emphasis on the "Superior Individual". Confucianism was radical in its time in suggesting that human beings were not merely helpless at the whim of either gods/spirits or unbending fate; they did not have to act as helpless infants pleading to the gods for succour. Instead, human beings had an active role to play in their own spiritual growth and could develop Virtue (which is not just "good morals" but rather qualities of magical power) that would allow them to play an active role in deciding their own destinies. In short, human beings are not just reactive to the universe, but can be proactive; they can guide their own transformation.

This book is not intended to be a guide to Confucian philosophy, and is only really concerned with its relationship to the I Ching, but suffice it to say that the core concept of significance relating to the I Ching is this idea of the "Superior Individual". It is the idea that a human being can choose, in the context of their surroundings, how to bring out the qualities of their "Superior" self, or alternately succumb to the qualities of their baser nature (the "Inferior Person"). These are not just ethical qualities; it was another great understanding of Confucianism that our lives are not just spiritual lives superimposed on a material shell, nor are they material lives separate from some out-there spiritual state, but rather that the Secular is Sacred. Thus, the qualities of the Superior Individual have an effect not only in the ethical sense in the conduct of our material lives (and how we shape our society) but also in the spiritual sense. Individuals who wish to experience true spiritual growth (and not just "blissed-out" dead-ends or delusions) must strive to become their best, to be as total as possible at whatever role they are meant to play in regular life. In so doing they bring their individual Will into harmony with the Will of Heaven. The true expansion of consciousness depends upon how capably and boldly one engages with one's life in the physical world.

Those who are familiar with the western-originated philosophy of Thelema and the elaboration on the subject of the True Will (embodied by the Law of Thelema: "Do what thou wilt shall be the whole of the Law/Love is the law, love under will") will no doubt take notice that there are certain strong similarities. This is unlikely to be a coincidence: Aleister Crowley (the "prophet" of Thelema) was a known Sinophile, and had travelled across China in 1905-1906 (where he may have first seen the I Ching in use; although there is some possibility he may have seen it earlier, in 1900 in San Francisco). He described the atmosphere of China as having "soaked into his soul". He also studied the translations that were available in his time of the "Sacred Writings of the East".

From a magical perspective, Confucian doctrine on the subject of the "Superior Individual" and the sacredness of the secular can be understood as Aeon of Osiris precursors to the core principles of the Aeon of Horus. This is part of why the I Ching remains exceedingly relevant to this day, and of particular interest to our own times and culture, where we are increasingly favourable to the idea of combining the sacred and the secular and in a spiritual path that calls on personal responsibility (rather than receiving "salvation" through either human or divine intercessors).

It is thus through the concept of the Superior Individual that the I Ching becomes a powerful tool for the development of the "Great Work" of discovering and doing our Will. Through this understanding, each hexagram of the I Ching not only describes a particular situation in time and space and how we can adapt to it, but also how in each of these situations we can best try to embody the virtues of the Superior Individual. With all due respect to Jung in his admiration of the I Ching, its primary purpose is not, in the style of psychology, to seek coincidental "synchronicity" to help us ease our mental well-being; but, in the style of true alchemy, to ultimately master Time and causality in order to transform ourselves into full embodiments of our human birthright. The Superior Individual is coterminous with the concept of Zarathustra's "Super-man"; that is, the next step in human evolution: what we are "becoming".

Shao Yung

A thousand years after Confucius' time, a blossoming of new Confucian thought began to emerge through a series of magnificent Chinese philosophers and mystics, for whom the I Ching was of particular significance in different ways. They elaborated on the already existing systems and developed new concepts; and while their work is not part of the direct canonical text of the I Ching in the way Confucius' commentaries are, they represent some of the last truly great breakthroughs in I Ching studies prior to the modern era.

The first, and greatest of these was Shao Yung. Like Confucius, he was famous in his own time as a great sage, and was attributed with great esoteric/magical power. Also like Confucius, he was unusual in that in spite of his fame he didn't have any kind of meaningful career in public office. He was a rebel in other ways as well: while most mainstream Confucians of his time were strong advocates of reading the I Ching only as a literal text on governance and rejected its use for divination, Shao Yung became the greatest advocate of studying the I Ching as a set of symbols that revealed mysteries of universal cosmology, and made almost-constant use of its divination techniques.

Most significantly, it was Shao Yung who began the process of revealing the numerological and mathematical mysteries inherent in the I Ching, and connected it to the five-element system of Chinese Astrology. He elaborated what came to be known as the "Earlier Heaven arrangement" of the trigrams, and demonstrated how the hexagrams of the I Ching formed a binary code. Based on these principles, he designed a system for utilizing the I Ching to cast hexagrams based on significant dates (one's "natal hexagrams" for an I Ching "birth chart", for example). This system is called the Plum Blossom Method (because it was revealed to Shao Yung under a plum tree), and it is explained further in Chapter Five. This is particularly relevant for the magical practitioner because it allows us to establish measurements of fixed moments in time, to utilize for the study of the self or the forecasting of auspicious moments for action in much the same way that we apply western astrology (but, in my own experience, with less hassle and more specific results).

Zhang Shi, Zhu Xi, and the Law of Change

In the century that followed Shao Yung's time, two other great Confucian masters had a dialogue that was significant to how we should understand the philosophy of the I Ching.

Zhang Shi was a Confucian philosopher who had given up an early career in the public service to become a hermit. He was renowned for his wisdom, and because of his fame, Zhu Xi, another Confucian philosopher who was about the same age but not yet as famous (though he would go on to become considerably more renowned) came to visit him. Legend has it they spent three days and three nights debating on the subject of "The Doctrine of the Mean", Confucius' teachings on harmony. Zhu Xi's previous teacher had strongly advocated the idea of "Wei-Fa", the "unmanifested mind" as being the most important aspect of reality; that is, that a mystic should focus more on the "unmanifested world", on contemplation of the metaphysical, and ignore the material world around him or view it only from the perspective of being a by-product of that metaphysical world. Zhang Shi, however, repudiated this idea. He explained that the idea of "Wei-Fa" was "the law of unchanging", the idea of trying to keep things separate; and that in isolation from the world this was impossible. Instead, he advocated "Yi-Fa", the "manifested state", as "the Law of Change".

Stillness, he argued, was impossible. You are always doing something, even when you are "doing" nothing. And any notion of equilibrium (as in wei-fa) was only a fantasy if it was not harmonized within the manifested world. To put it more simply: if your spiritual practice divorces you from the physical, then you are engaging in a kind of make-believe. If your practice is found within the physical and is enhanced by the physical, then it is productive and leads to growth. We are in a constant state of Change, and by accepting this and living it out in a meditative way, we gain awareness and transformation. Rather than trying to separate from Change to achieve meditation or stillness, we must seek to manifest "stillness in doing".

Zhu Xi was convinced, and went on to elaborate this understanding: Wei-Fa is the "life force" and Yi-Fa is our manifestation, how we operate in time and space. Of these, he concludes, we have to venerate Wei-Fa by expressing it within Yi-Fa. His great synthesis was to understand that in fact, the true path to wisdom is not in rejecting the Wei-Fa but in understanding that the Wei-Fa exists incipient within the Yi-Fa; these forces are constantly recreating one another. "In a flash," he expressed, "the manifest is just gone (that is, changes) and the unmanifest is coming forth. There is no break between the two" (Ching, 2000). Human beings can only find the Wei-Fa in harmony with the Yi-Fa, they are the same Reality.

Students of western magick, and particularly Thelema, can perhaps understand the relationship between these ideas and the philosophy described in the Liber AL vel Legis, the Book of the Law; a profoundly significant spiritual text received by Aleister Crowley in 1904, dictated to him by his Augoeides ("higher self", or "Holy Guardian Angel"), Aiwass. There, we are informed that "The Khabs is in the Khu, not the Khu in the Khabs" (AL I:8); wherein "khabs" is an Egyptian term for "star" (the source of light) while "khu" is our manifest being. Thus the message is similar: contrary to the Manichean line of thought present in so many religions and philosophies, where we are called upon to either reject the body and the material world, or, at best, treat it as nothing more than a meaningless by-product or unimportant shell of some faraway spiritual reality, we are being told (by the Liber AL and by the Law of Change alike!) that our physical reality is the only valid field of action through which we are able to discover ourselves as "stars". Enlightenment, Magick, or Spirituality are not things that we can connect to by ignoring reality; they depend upon the discovery of reality, and this begins with working with what is directly in front of us. Our bodies, our minds, our emotions, our physical surroundings, our relationships, our actions of all types, are the very magical "working tools" through which we can uncover, connect to, and express our True Will.

Zhang Shi was so inspired by his meeting with Zhu Xi that he gave up his hermit life and returned to public service. By the time of his death he was a provincial governor. Zhu Xi's public life was not as glamorous: he made the mistake of openly denouncing incompetence and corruption in the imperial bureaucracy, was denied promotions, eventually stripped of office, and executed. However, after his death his writings went on to be so influential that his figure was officially rehabilitated. He was made into one of the philosophers venerated at the Confucian Temple, and is revered as one of the "Twelve Eminent Philosophers" of Confucian thought; the only one, in fact, not to have been a direct disciple of Confucius. Thus he is considered the greatest teacher of "Neo-Confucianism" (the post eighth-century renaissance/reformation of Confucian teaching).

Curiously, Zhu Xi is known for having chosen to focus and comment upon Confucius' other teachings rather than the I Ching, which in his own time was the central text of Confucian interest. But while he wrote less on that subject than any of the other Confucian classics, what he did have to say about it was of extreme importance. In fact, it is his description of how to perform divination that became the accepted standard, the instructions still used in most books and translations to this day.

In surviving letters to Zhang Shi, Zhu Xi commented that the central way to learn from the I Ching is by its practice in actual divination, rather than just the study of its symbolism; this idea was in direct contradiction to what the mainstream scholars of the time advocated, as they tended to treat divination with the suspicion of being mere superstition. Zhu Xi took this same attitude to the other Confucian teachings, that they were not just a philosophy to be thought about, but something that had to be applied in one's actions. This is clearly a result of his revelation about the nature of Yi-Fa and Wei-Fa (it also hearkened back to Shao Yung, who was likewise a rebellious advocate of divination practice, and who Zhu Xi greatly admired). The cultivation of Virtue ("Te", the magical power of the conscious individual) was more important to create social progress than knowledge alone. He also firmly expressed that all individuals could cultivate Virtue through practice, regardless of their background, as they all had the unmanifest life force within them. In other words, "Every man and every woman is a star" (AL I:3). He expressly stated that the practice of divination was essential for individuals to be able to understand how to develop their particular Virtue in response to their own situations.

He stated, in accordance with his view on the Law of Change, that the nature of I Ching divination worked not by "fortune-telling" in the sense of seeing some intractable vision of a future event (which is indeed how common fortune-tellers, both then and now, often wish to see it), nor by some kind of supernatural gift available only to a chosen few (which again, was the claim of some "Taoist masters" then, and is the assertion of some "psychics" now), but rather by being able to give a careful and precise measurement of Time in this present space. Within the present, future directions were already "incipient" and could thus be examined the way one could examine the map of a territory to know where he could choose to go. He also stated that this meant that the ability to skilfully interpret the result of an I Ching casting depended neither on one's erudite knowledge of Confucian philosophy (fortunately for us), nor on some kind of supernatural boon, but on one's level of "integrity". All divinations show patterns, he stated, but one will only be able to plainly judge the incipiencies found therein to the degree to which one has perfected his own integrity, removing the selfish fantasies of his mind's eye; someone who has not cultivated sincerity will be unable to accurately judge even the clearest oracle.

The Map of Time

The I Ching is thus a map of time. It is not surprising that it fascinated the great innovators in quantum physics. Likewise, the psychedelic thinker Terrence McKenna was correct in understanding that the I Ching works by mapping what he called "novelty", though his claim to have been able to somehow definitively chart it proved to be nothing more than a fantasy of his own "mind's eye". Perhaps the most impressive discoveries in the I Ching since at least Shao Yung's time have come from western mathematicians, who have applied Boolean algebra to the I Ching, and discovered that the sixty four hexagrams of the I Ching map out into a "Boolean lattice" (Schoter, 2005). This demonstrates how the I Ching can be mathematically projected into a sixth dimensional hyper-geometrical prismatic figure. That is to say, some of the hexagrams existing within other hexagrams are meant to reflect hyper-dimensionality. The I Ching is a way of taking a measurement of time and its projected course, through a six-dimensional mathematical code projected into our four-dimensional range of perception of space and time.

So together, the hexagrams are a conceptual "drawing" of time itself in the same way we might draw distance. From the point of view of a sixth-dimensional universe, time would look like a physical object (just like, conversely, if we existed in a second-dimensional universe depth would not have solid form). Imagine if someone could take a picture of you, doing everything you've ever done, but all at once: from that perspective all those different "yous" would look like a single solid object, a long winding string weaving along the other dimensions of depth, height, and width in relative space. This is difficult even now to wrap our heads around, but it means that the hexagrams of the I Ching collectively are as much a "physical map" of Time as one could have a physical map of, say, Norway.

While the mathematical/scientific understandings expressed here are very modern, this same concept was already present in the doctrine of Yi-Fa, and Zhu Xi's understanding of it; he said that "incipience" is "the imperceptible beginning of a movement". What he is describing is a waveform of potential futures, about to collapse into the present. He said "between activity and stillness, substance and function, suddenly in the space of an instant there is the beginning of the actual pattern, and the auspicious and inauspicious omens of the multitudinous phenomena" (Smith, K., et al. 1990).

This is the importance of the concept of Yi-Fa, the Law of Change, and how it makes the difference in practice that allows us to become skillful at understanding reality and our own Will (as the expression of how we must act within reality at this moment in time). It is only by avoiding the temptations of the "Inferior Person", by getting out of our own way, that we will be able to capture that instant of incipience, and obtain a clear vision of where the map of time is directing us.

"The I Ching is Not About You"

When you look at the weather report to see if it is going to rain so that you know whether to go to the park or not, you are "consulting" the weather report, but that doesn't mean that the weather report is about you.

So let's look at this concept from the perspective of I Ching practice. If you are acting as what Confucius would call "the superior man" (what in western practice could be called the "True Will"; the Individuality, and thus I have termed it the "Superior Individual"), then an I Ching casting can certainly be done to ask about anything: money, romance, work, whether a meeting will go well, anything at all. But whatever you are asking, the underlying question the Superior Individual asks is not "what should I do" but "what is the best thing to do?"

So in that sense, also, it is not about "you". It is not about your lesser nature, or about doing what you want or getting what you want, but about trying to get a "weather forecast" of reality itself (time and space), and then ascertain from that what is truly the best thing that can be done in conformity to your Will, regardless of pettier concepts or notions. Every I Ching casting is, in that sense, a readout of how close the consultant is to his Will, and what needs to be done next to continue to perform the "Great Work" of embodying the "Superior Individual". This is the way of Yi-Fa.

Chapter Two

How to Use the I Ching

The first and most crucial piece of advice for "using" the I Ching is ridiculously commonsensical, but is nevertheless something many would-be I Ching practitioners seem to fail to consider: if you want to develop a good working relationship with the I Ching, you should read the entire I Ching.

It is surprising how many people have tried to make regular use of the I Ching, performing I Ching divination, without actually having read the text from cover-to-cover. This is just as ill-advised as trying to use the Tarot for Tarot readings without first looking at all of the cards and getting to know them!

It may be that the excess of commentaries and the sometimes-complicated language used in other versions of the I Ching have acted as a barrier, causing some practitioners to experience some intimidation when it comes to actually reading the whole of the text. Nevertheless, this is an essential condition to getting to know and understand the I Ching.

In addition to this, it is a good idea for a practitioner to spend time considering the trigrams, and how they interact with each other. Look at the lines that make up a trigram: observe whether it has two broken lines, or two solid lines (or is completely broken or solid), and how this compares to the other trigrams. When you compare two trigrams, is only one line different, or two, or are all three different (making the trigrams direct opposites to each other)? How does this relate to the symbolism associated with that trigram? Consider how those symbols interact: what images do they evoke in you to imagine Air in the bottom and Earth on the top (or vice-versa); or Sun on the top and The World on the bottom? Do the two constituent forces together sound complementary or oppositional? Do they look complementary side-by-side, or not so much? All of these are things to consider and keep coming back to.

Even as you continue to read the I Ching, and contemplate the trigrams (and you should continue to come back to these practices for as long as you intend to keep using the I Ching), you can begin to perform divination with the I Ching.

Like all divination, the I Ching does not so much predict the future, as it takes a really good look at the present: understanding the present, what forces affect it, allows one to get a good idea not only of where one is, but of where one is going. It is important while performing I Ching readings to remember that the reading is a kind of diagnosis of your current space-time; the relationship between your being in this moment and existence.

The literal translation of the word "I Ching" is "The Book of Changes". This is because the I Ching system recognizes that existence is a constant state of flow and flux, nothing is ever static for very long; you are always moving, life is always moving around you. So just as two three-line trigrams unite into a six-line hexagram, that hexagram is in the process of changing, slowly or quickly, into another hexagram. Most readings will have one or more "changing lines", points of particular importance in the current situation because they represent where change is happening. These are lines that are presently weak but about to become strong, or presently strong but about to become weak; they will change the trigram they belong to into a different trigram, one element becomes another, and the overall situation evolves into a new hexagram. Thus any I Ching reading will (usually) involve three stages of interpretation: first, of the hexagram that represents the situation as it currently stands; second, of the changing lines and those specific details that are most important in the present situation; and third, the "future" hexagram that represents where the situation is moving toward.

It is possible for a hexagram to have no "changing lines"; this is a sign of a situation that is particularly stable for the moment, with little motion in the short term or opportunity to change.

I Ching Reading Methods

There are several methods for creating an I Ching hexagram. In the oldest methods of generating a hexagram, turtle shells or bones of various kinds were used to divine the component lines. These were cast over a fire and the lines interpreted based on the cracks which formed. This was the main form of divination used by the Shang Dynasty, prior to the time of King Wen.

King Wen, and the new Zhou Dynasty that descended from him, mainly used a counting system utilizing bunches of yarrow stalks. This system is complex by modern standards, but it was revolutionary at the time because of its precision, its uses of probability, and because it meant that there was no ambiguity about the hexagram cast (unlike the turtle-shell method, where often the hexagram had to be guessed at from vague sets of cracks). It removed the need for excessively complex ritual; the yarrow-stalk method and the setting down of the I Ching in a text format removing the need for second-hand intervention from professional augurs. It was an example of a leap forward in "magical technology".

Later, an even simpler method developed, making use of coins. This is considerably quicker than the yarrow-stalk method, but it removes the sophistication of probability (the odds of getting lines of either type, or changing lines of either type, are equal), and is generally less accurate as a measurement of the precise moment in time and space (though clearly still functional enough that many people have used it to their benefit). Both in different historical periods, and in modern times, some practitioners have made use of more intuitive methods to create an I Ching reading.

For the purpose of this text, I will describe a new method that is simple but allows one to generate hexagrams using the same probabilities for lines as the ancient "yarrow stalk" method. I will also include the popular "three coin" method, and an even simpler very quick "six coin" method (similar to the method used by Aleister Crowley; who derived his own way of generating a hexagram due to his lack of access to any information about the traditional methods). I will also include an example of how to generate hexagrams intuitively. Finally, in Chapter Five I will include eleventh-century philosopher Shao Yung's "Plum Blossom Method" for generating hexagrams based on dates and numbers.

All methods begin with the same essential process: in the first place, it is strongly advised to present a question to the I Ching. This question can be almost anything, but it is often advisable (especially for beginners) to present the question in the form of a question answerable as "yes/no" or "good/bad": "Should I do x" or "is it a good idea to do y" are good ways to frame a question. Generally it is better to ask this way than to present the question in a garbled way with conflicting options (e.g., "should I do x or y"?), because this divided attention can sometimes lead to muddled answers. In fact, more than half the battle of learning how to use the I Ching effectively involves knowing how to formulate the right question.

It is a very good idea to make a "ritual" out of an I Ching casting, as making a ritual out of the process will put you into a particular kind of perceptual state that assists clarity in experiencing and understanding the casting. At the same time, you should also take care not to make this ritual excessively complicated; the I Ching is meant to be practical and workable.

The traditional ritual involved with the I Ching involves first washing your hands before you begin, as a purification. Then light a stick of incense and take out your divination devices: your sticks or coins or whatever other instruments you use should be kept in some kind of simple but special container; wrapped in cloth or kept in a small box. There is a ritualistic element to freeing the devices, setting you in a frame of mind that you are now starting to enter a "ritual space" in your consciousness. You then take the instruments in hand, and perform three brief bows (what were once called "Kow-tows"), as a sign of reverence and to further the mental and intuitive preparation; then circle the instruments around the smoke of the incense stick three times.

After this, you should breathe into the divination devices as you speak your question out loud; creating a magical connection, a link between yourself, through the question, to your tools. Then cast the devices and begin to record the results.

Note that none of these steps have any essential power; they are all meant simply to help you to get into the proper mental state of attention, to send a message to yourself that you are about to do something important that requires you to show up and be aware. None of them are strictly required; if you wished to, you could do a reading in a busy street with dirty hands while smoking a cigarette. The essential part is to put one's self into the proper inner space. For that reason, what is very strongly recommended is at the very least to pause and spend a few moments in silent meditation, paying attention to your posture and breathing, before beginning the reading. If you wish, you could incorporate elements of your personal practice into this preparation: you could perform a brief invocation in the way you are accustomed, or you can bring your guru to mind, or visualize a mandala, or vibrate sacred words, before you begin.

Method I: The "Four Stave" Method

This is a new method, in print here for the first time that I know of (though I have also shared it with private discussion groups). I have devised this method myself, after having felt dissatisfaction with the imperfect mirroring of change from the more popular "three coin" method; while at the same time finding the complexities of the traditional counting method (using fifty yarrow stalks) to often be too impractical. While it is called "four staves" and my own preference is to use four wooden sticks, you could in fact use any four two-sided objects; these can be coins, or flat sticks, or anything else, where the two sides are distinguishable from one another (coins with a "head" and "tail", for example, or sticks that have a mark on one side). In my own case, I use four carpenter's pencils (which are two-sided) and have marked one side of each with a black line to delineate the "Yang" side.

If you are a western magician, you might wish to "consecrate" these staves before you use them for the first time, by performing an invocation of Mercurial energy and anointing the staves with Oil of Abramelin, or some other sacred substance.

To perform a reading, begin with the ritual procedure delineated above.

You should be prepared with paper and pen (to note the results), and then toss the devices. For simplicity's sake, assume one side of the device is the "Yang" side, and the other is the "Yin" side; If you are using something other than coins, it's a good idea to mark only one side to allow for quick and easy distinction as to which side is which.

When you throw the devices, you have to see how they each come up:

- if all four come up Yin, the result is a broken changing line. Draw a split line and put a mark or an "x" next to it, to note it is a changing line.

- if three come up Yin (and one Yang): the result is a broken line. Draw a split line.

- if they are tied (2 and 2) you have to look at the one that fell furthest to your left:

  —if that symbol is a Yin: the result is a broken line (draw a split line);

  —if that symbol is a Yang: the result is a solid changing line (draw it and put a mark or an 'x' next to it, to note that it is a changing line);

  —if three come up Yang (and one Yin), OR if all four come up Yang: the result is a solid line. Draw a straight line on your page;

As usual, you do this six times to generate the hexagram. The lines are drawn from bottom to top, so the first line you generate should be the lowest (first) of the six, the last one you generate will be the highest.

The reason this method is preferable to the "three coin method" is that in that latter method there is an equal chance of getting a solid or broken line; and an equal (lesser) chance of getting a solid changing or broken changing line. But in the "Four Staves" method it is most rare to get a broken changing line (1/16 chance); slightly less rare to get a solid changing line (3/16); less rare still to get a solid line (5/16), and most common of all to get a broken line (7/16). These odds match those of the oldest method of I Ching divination, the complicated counting method of fifty yarrow stalks. The odds with that method are almost exactly the same as in this method, and this is important because this method more accurately reflects the probabilities of Change. It is more probable in reality that something will be in a state of weakness than in a state of strength; and more probable that something strong will weaken, than that something weak will be strengthening.

This is the nature of reality; so by using this method you get the most accurate approximation of the laws of nature.

Method II: The "Three Coin" Method

Perhaps the most popular method for creating an I Ching casting involves using three coins. Any three coins can be used, but these should if at all possible be special coins that you have permanently set aside to use for I Ching readings. For the sake of balance, it is strongly advised that all three coins be the same type of coin (the same size and shape). Each coin should have two clearly distinct sides, which for the purpose of description will here be described as "heads" and "tails" (if the coin you use is not clearly identifiable as such, you should designate one side as the "head" and the other as the "tail").

- With paper and writing implement ready, you should hold all three coins in your hands for a moment, then drop or gently toss them in front of you:

  —if two out of three coins come up "heads", that is a regular "Yang" (solid) line;

  —if two out of three coins come up "tails", that is a regular "Yin" (broken) line;

  —if all three coins come up "heads", that is a "changing Yang" line (this is a solid line with an "x" drawn beside it, to note that it is changing);

  —if all three coins come up "tails", that is a "changing Yin" line (this is a broken line with an "x" drawn beside it, to note that it is changing).

- Repeat this process five more times, to finish drawing six lines, one above the other, until you've drawn a full six-line hexagram (consisting of two trigrams, one above the other).

Method III: The "Six Coin" Method

This method is less sophisticated than the first method, but can be used if one wants a faster drawing or to answer a simpler question:

- take six coins (or alternately, six flat sticks with one side marked somehow to differentiate the "Yang" side from the "Yin" side);

- toss the coins (or sticks) in front of you, and then line them up in order of distance: the coin that fell closest to you is the "base" of the hexagram, the next-closest is the second line, the next one after that the third line, etc. until you have created a hexagram of six lines, giving you a simple hexagram to refer to your question.

This method does not inherently produce a hexagram with any changing lines; you can include one or more changing lines by making one of the six coins different from the others (meaning that coin will mark the "changing line"), or by putting a mark on one of the coins or sticks to indicate the same. Alternately, you can use an intuitive method to determine the changing line(s) if necessary.

Method IV: The Intuitive Methods

There are several less structured methods to perform an I Ching casting. One simple way is to have sixty-four cards with a hexagram drawn on each; drawing one at random will provide you with the hexagram to answer your question (optionally, a second card drawn can represent the "future" hexagram, with the differences between the two hexagrams revealing which lines from the original hexagram drawn are the changing lines). This system will be very far from reflecting the nature of the Changes, but it is a favourite of fortune-tellers in both Asia and the West.

If you have neither coins nor sticks nor cards, you can use less orthodox methods of determining a hexagram. If you are in a crowded area, you could observe the people that pass by you: if a man walks by, it indicates a Yang (solid) line; while a woman walking by indicates a Yin (broken) line. You can make use of some particular characteristic predetermined at the start of the reading to ascertain if any of the lines are changing lines (for example, if instead of an adult man or woman, it's a boy or girl who walks past you). Alternately, look at a watch: use the first digit of the "minutes" of the present time to determine the changing line, wherein each ten-minute block after the hour would represent a value of 1 (so for example, 9:45 pm would mean the changing line is 5).

If you have great confidence in your intuition, you could simply choose to empty your thoughts until the image of a solid or a broken line appears to you, and draw that as your first line; then repeat the process for the second to sixth lines; likewise using your intuition to envision the changing line or lines.

In addition to his numerological "plum blossom" method, the I Ching master Shao Yung often favoured the pure observation of nature to select his component trigrams. He would look around and choose for his hexagram the trigrams that the vision before him intuitively provided. For example, you might be sitting outside and when you begin to meditate the first sensation you take note of is someone lighting a cigarette; thus you select the Fire trigram for the lower part of your hexagram; then you feel a light breeze on your face, and thus select Air for your second trigram. Alternately you might see someone unloading a crate, and this reminds you of the Earth trigram, then you see someone almost stumble as he walks down a step, and this reminds you of the pit-like quality of the Moon trigram. This type of exercise requires both a strong level of meditative intuition (trance) and significant familiarity with the correspondences of the various trigrams; however, it can also prove to be a very useful way of familiarizing yourself with the trigrams and their elemental qualities in action.

A Note On Probabilities

It is my position that the differences in the above methods for casting a hexagram are significant, in terms of probability for determining both lines and changing lines. It is my feeling that Method I is the most trustworthy system, because these probabilities most accurately reflect the nature of change in reality (which is what the I Ching attempts to reflect). In nature, it is more common for the strong to weaken than for the weak to strengthen, and this power of entropy is what is reflected in the mathematical odds of the Four Stave method (indeed, as in the ancient Yarrow Stalk method). In the Three-coin and Six-coin methods, it is equally possible to get Yin or Yang; it is a randomness that is less reflective of reality.

Nevertheless, the I Ching is trustworthy enough in its symbolic strength that whichever method you use, you will be able to obtain wisdom that reflects some kind of insight, assuming that you allow your mind and your fears to get out of the way. This will of course have some degree of imperfection (regardless of the method used) relative to how well, or how poorly, you get out of your own way.

How to Read the Hexagrams

Each I Ching hexagram corresponds to a single chapter of the I Ching text.

Once you have determined the hexagram (and changing lines), look up the appropriate chapter of the I Ching that matches this hexagram (a table is provided below for quick reference to the chapters, by cross-referencing the component trigrams).

Once you have found the appropriate section, the first step is to look at the title of the section, and consider the nature of the trigrams that make up that hexagram: which trigrams are involved, which is below and which above. After that, read the basic description of the hexagram. You may also wish to study the Commentary and the advice provided regarding how this hexagram relates to the performance of the "Great Work".

After the basic description, six oracles are provided, which correspond to the six lines (remember: they are read from bottom-to-top, so that "line 1" is the line at the very bottom of the hexagram, and "line 6" is the line at the very top of the hexagram). For the purpose of the reading, you should read and consider *only* those individual lines that were marked as "changing lines" in your reading. These changing lines are usually the most essential part of the reading; while the general description explains your present situation, the "changing lines" describe the specific interaction of yourself and the situation. In other words, what you should be particularly careful to do or to avoid, or how the general situation affects you. Sometimes, the meaning of the main text of the hexagram, and the meaning of the changing lines seem to be opposite to each other; in these cases, you should consider the main text line as referring to the overall situation, while the changing line to your particular situation. After all, there could be times when the overall situation around you is bad and yet things are going to be beneficial to you in particular, or where the situation in general is prosperous and yet through accident or error you cannot gain from it.

You may have more than one changing line, or you may have none at all. You can generally visualize the overall reading as going in a kind of chronological order, where the main hexagram represents the foundation of the situation, the changing line or lines the step or steps you are going through in the situation, and the "future hexagram" the further development of the situation. At times, castings with multiple changing lines might also seem to have contradictory changing lines. In these cases, it is important to remember that the lines are not describing things that are happening all at once; the lower lines represent earlier events, and the higher lines later events.

After studying the changing lines, draw a new hexagram from the old one, where any line in the old hexagram that was marked as a "changing line" is now changed into its new form. For example, if the lower trigram of your hexagram was the "Moon" trigram ☵ where the second line was a "changing line", in the new hexagram you draw that trigram will now be changed into a "World" trigram. ☰

Looking up the section for this new hexagram, read its title and consider its component elements. After this, you would typically read its general description and commentary only (though there are some situations where you might also be called on to read specific changing lines; see below). This "future" hexagram describes where the situation is going, giving you an impression of the longer term developments that will arise, and possibly a general idea of the ultimate resolution of your question.

In I Ching tradition, the number of changing lines you have affects what should be read, and allows you to determine which particular part of the overall reading represents the "centre", that part of the casting that marks the present or the most urgent thing to attend to (with all that comes before that "centre" being previous developments, and all that comes after being later developments).

In the reading, if you have:

No Moving line:	then read the Main Hexagram Text only.
1 Moving Line:	then read the Main Hexagram Text, the Moving Line, and the Future Hexagram Text; and the Moving Line is the "centre".
2 Moving Lines:	then read the Main Hexagram Text, both Moving Lines, and the Future Hexagram Text; and the UPPER Moving Line is the "centre".

3 Moving Lines:	then read the Main Hexagram Text, all three Moving Lines, and the Future Hexagram Text; and the MIDDLE Moving Line is the "centre".
4 Moving Lines:	then read the Main Hexagram Text, the four Moving Lines, the Future Hexagram Text, and the two lines from the Future Hexagram that were unmoving (for example, if you get a hexagram with lines 1-4 moving; then you will read lines 5 and 6 of the Future Hexagram). Of these, the LOWER Future Hexagram Line is the "centre".
5 Moving Lines:	then read the Main Hexagram Text, all five Moving Lines, the Future Hexagram Text, and the unmoving Future Hexagram Line; and the single unmoving Future Hexagram Line is the "centre".
6 Moving Lines:	then read the Main Hexagram Text, all six Moving Lines, and the Future Hexagram Text; and the Future Hexagram Text is the "centre".

(Note that in all cases, as well as the main text description of a hexagram, one can also read the image description, the commentary, and the instructions on the Superior Individual, here titled "the Great Work").

All of the above describes the basic way you would read an I Ching casting, and it is how you begin. As you develop there are other aspects to what you are doing that you'll want to look at, however, it is not good to overburden yourself at the beginning. Make certain that you have a firm grasp of the fundamental method before delving into other details. Later on, you may want to contemplate the structure of the hexagrams you cast: look at the lines, which line is where, understand why that makes certain things good or bad. Look at and contemplate the image evoked by the component trigrams (both the "official" one described in the book and other ways you could imagine those two elements combining to create an image). You will also want to look at the "nuclear hexagrams" involved, as well as the "opposite", "overturned" and "reversed" hexagrams; you will find more information on this in the later chapters of the book.

A Guide to Common Phrases and Words in I Ching Hexagrams

There are several words or phrases that are repeated in multiple I Ching Hexagrams. These have particular meanings, and the following is an attempt to list and explain some of them:

- **"Abyss"**: A profound pit. The Abyss symbolizes darkness, and being stuck or lost. It can be literal but also has the symbolic connotation of having become trapped in a place of profound ignorance, blocked off from the Great Work. It is the negative aspect of the subconscious, the mental fears and conditioning that block our ability to hear our True Will.

- **"Base (people)"**: The opposite of "Superior men" or "the Good", the "Base" refers to the class of people who are of poor moral quality (the "Inferior Person"); vile or ignorant people, people who are treacherous, crude or violent. From the perspective of the Great Work, it can also relate to one's own inferior and limited self.

- **"Beasts"**: The term "beasts" (which could also be translated as "animals") refers literally to wild animals. In several hexagrams there are references to generic "beasts" being hunted, or hunting someone, or lurking dangerously (for example, in the battlefields, in line 5 of hexagram #7, "the Army"). However, these "beasts" are often also an allegory for uncultured, untrustworthy people. Spiritually, they can be understood to represent those who operate on base instinct and ignorance.

- **"Blame/Fault/Error":** When misfortune occurs, it is usually a product of your own choices leading directly or inadvertently to that misfortune. "Blame", "Fault", or "Error" appearing in a reading refers to a situation where your actions were particularly and directly responsible for the misfortune that has come to pass. On the other hand "No blame" or "no fault" means that the misfortune was unavoidable as part of the flow of things and could not be helped.

  Sometimes, "no blame" implies that if you take a particular course, you will be able to avoid being badly judged by others. From a Confucian perspective, the question of "blame" or "fault" is particularly important, because "blame" is considered to be a kind of karma; the purpose of life in Confucian thought is to accumulate much "Virtue" while accruing as little "blame" (both of which are seen as measurable substances); the ratio of one's Virtue vs. Blame will affect the condition of one's afterlife.

- **"Blessed/Blessing":** Being "blessed" or receiving a "blessing" refers to good fortune that comes along unexpectedly, or is not due to your own direct actions.

- **"Carriage":** On a literal level this relates to the standard mode of transporting people and goods. But usually this has a metaphorical sense of being the "vehicle" for one's efforts. In some hexagrams of the I Ching, we are warned that the wheel or axle of the carriage will be broken; this implies lesser or greater crises which halt progress.

  In some cases, the Carriage is related to the notion of public office; a Superior Individual may gain a position which allows him to travel the land in a carriage and do good. In at least one line (line 1 of hexagram 22), we are advised to step out of our carriage and walk for ourselves; implying that we don't need to rely (in that situation) on an outer vehicle or method.

Mystically, the "Carriage" relates to the concept of the "vehicle" as a "dharma", as a system of practice that can be used to make change in accordance to the Will. It is reminiscent to the trump card of the Tarot known as the Chariot.

- **"Courtship":** In a literal sense, the elaborate social rituals undertaken when seeking a wife or husband. In a mystical sense, this term in a hexagram can refer to the practice of magical ritual for the purpose of uniting to one's True Will. It is in a similar fashion that in western magick we see the practice of the "knowledge and conversation of the Holy Guardian Angel" referred to in the context of a love affair.

- **"Criminals"/"Rebels"/ "Evil-doers":** In the I Ching, these terms refer to those who are generically acting against either the natural course of things, or opposing your own Will if you are acting naturally.

- **"Cross the (great) River":** Crossing the river generally refers to a journey, going somewhere as part of trying to achieve your goals. "Cross the River" can refer to a short journey, while "Cross the Great River" will usually refer to a longer journey. "Don't cross the river" or similar phrases suggest that you should not go anywhere, and usually that it will be better to wait and bide your time, or to let the solution come to you. Such a description can be in reference to a symbolic journey as well.

- **"Dragon":** In Chinese Mythology, Dragons were celestial beings, sky-spirits of tremendous power. They were symbolic of the creative force, and a powerful masculine symbol. They were generally benevolent, but could be ferocious. They represent a force that is bound only by itself, that can only stop itself but cannot be stopped by anything else in nature; thus the Dragon is symbolic of the True Will.

It appears that in ancient Chinese religious practices, Dragons were thought to reside inside caves deep in the earth; and when they awoke and chose to emerge, the heavens thundered at their presence and thus caused rain to fall. Ancient rituals were performed to seek to call forth the Dragons, to awaken them at the right time, and for the rains to assist in causing abundant crops (the line descriptions of hexagram #1 refers directly to this tradition). In this way, the Dragon is connected to fertility rights, and (from the symbolic interpretation of the same) to sexual alchemy.

- **"Foreign/Foreigners/Outsiders":** This refers to people or groups outside of your normal circle. It can mean someone who is literally foreign, but it can also signify someone who is merely a stranger or from some other social group, or even someone who represents a set of interests outside your own.

- **"Gain":** The term "Gain" in the I Ching means that you advance in your goals.

- **"Gentle Success":** This means things will go well, but either slowly or only in relatively moderate measure.

- **"Goal":** Having a goal means having some kind of organized plan or destination. If it is "good to have a goal", that means that it is a good policy to be organized and have a plan for where you want to go. If it is "bad to have a goal", or "no goals are possible", it means that at this time trying to make plans is ill-advised because the situation is either too stuck or too chaotic.

- **"Good Luck/Bad Luck":** Having "luck" or "good luck" means that there is good fortune due to your own actions being natural and going with the flow of existence; it is lucky, but because of your choices. "Bad luck" (or the more extreme "disaster") refers to misfortune, that sometimes appears to be unexpected or not your fault, and is sometimes unavoidable, but is ultimately a result of the path you are taking. "Bad luck" is connected to the concept of "blame" or "Error"; some lines will explicitly state that a situation is "bad luck, but no blame", suggesting that the unlucky situation is not due to any deviation on your part from your true Will. If this is not explicitly stated, it can be assumed that the bad luck is in some way related to such a deviation.

- **"Hunter"/"prey":** This terminology appears in several hexagrams; it can sometimes refer to a hunt (possibly a Royal hunt), or at other times it is a metaphor for a military campaign, where the hunter is a general and the prey an enemy or rebel force. In esoteric terms, the "hunter" represents one who is seeking to direct his Will to a certain effect. If the prey is "lost", then it is a sign that what he sought to accomplish doesn't come to pass, usually because he did not concentrate his Will sufficiently.

- **"Law"**: There are many references to "law" or "laws" in the I Ching. In some cases, it talks about the "Law of Heaven", in others, the law of the King or "rulers of old". In some hexagrams we are told that it is a "good time for legal processes".

  From a magical context, Law here refers to the concept of dharma, the teaching; not in the sense of some specific teaching designed by human beings, but to the fundamental laws of Reality that govern all things and that all specific teachings based on Truth draw upon. To engage in legal processes can be a reference to using the dharma to rectify problems, most often problems related to the "Inferior Person" within yourself.

- **"King"**: See "Superior Individual".

- **"Marriage"**: The word marriage might refer to literal marriage, but it can also refer to any kind of union: romance, a partnership, people coming together. Many I Ching hexagrams refer to a "damsel" (or "virgin"), that is, an unmarried woman; usually in reference to courtship and potential marriage. In this case, the damsel can also metaphorically represent the object of one's desires, including the mystical longing for a transcendent experience of reintegrating matter with spirit.

- **"Official"**: Someone in a position of official authority. See also, "public office".

- **"Ox/Ox-hide"**: The ox is seen as a sign of both strength and prosperity. Gaining or losing an ox means gaining or losing prosperity. Something made of "ox hide" is particularly strong and resistant.

- **"Prince"**: See "Superior Individual".

- **"Public Office"**: There are several lines in the hexagrams that refer to "public office"; at times warning you not to seek it out, at times suggesting you will receive said office, or at times instructing you on how to conduct yourself in it. At the literal level, this refers to positions of authority and recognition. In a deeper sense, it refers to how "public" you make yourself in terms of your expression of your Will. To "misuse" public office is to squander or corrupt what you had at first accomplished through your true Will; that is, to lose sight of what constitutes right conduct in your current situation.

- **"Pushing":** This word refers to making a continued effort. It means to act with concentration.

- **"Rain":** In the symbolism of the I Ching, rain was brought by Dragons flying through the sky. The Dragon is associated with the Heaven trigram and the solid Yang line. The esoteric symbolism of "rain" is that of Change, of transformation. Thus, there are times, when "rain falls" or "rain pours" at suitable moments, where the rain presages great prosperity. At other times, rain can represent change in the sense of "crisis", potential danger or difficulty that destabilizes order. But even in those circumstances, in the longer term "rain" provides opportunities for renewal and growth.

- **"Right Pushing"/"Pushing Rightly"/etc.:** This phrase means making a continued effort, but in a "right" direction. Generally this means acting in harmony with the natural flow of things, and also pushing for a noble or proper purpose, acting in accordance with the true Will.

- **"Sacrifice":** The term "sacrifice" in the I Ching has two meanings. In the first case, it refers to performing proper rituals; this can include engaging in meditation, divination, or spiritual/magical rituals, but it can also mean going through the right and correct processes or taking proper steps. Second, "sacrifice" usually also means having to give something up. In ancient China, ritual practices usually involved some serious costs and expenditures. The oracle may not necessarily refer to money, however. It could be a sacrifice of time, or of more abstract things. To "sacrifice blood" means to make a particularly serious "sacrifice", getting involved in very serious processes or giving up something very important.

- **"Seek the Superior Individual"/"See a Great Man":** This can refer to literally going to, or seeking advice or help from, a "Great Man". However, it can also be an injunction to seek out the Superior Individual within yourself (see the entry on "Superior Individual" for more information).

- **"Shame/Shameful":** In the I Ching, when something brings "shame" or is "shameful" it implies public embarrassment, usually because some socially improper behaviour will become too visible to others. However, the I Ching often implies that this is not a very serious problem, and often it may be worth the embarrassing situation if what you are doing is right or helpful, or for the sake of the Great Work.

- **"Superior Individual"/"Great Man":** The "Superior Individual" in the I Ching can refer to two things: a man of great importance or powerful position in relation to the question asked, or a man of great moral quality and wisdom, someone who is at one with the Tao, and follows their True Will. Often it means both at the same time.

In a reading, "seeing a great man" means going to get help or advice from someone who matches this description. In standard translation, the I Ching actually says "the Superior Man" (or more accurately in a technically literal sense "the (male) royal heir"), but it is evident that by no means does a "Superior Man" have to be of the male gender. As such and in accordance with the times, I have chosen to use the non-gendered "Superior Individual". This was done not only to be inclusive to those not of the male gender, but also because it expresses the concept of the "Individuality" (the "higher self", one's true Nature) as opposed to the "Personality" (the hodgepodge of influences, sometimes referred to as "the ego" by western meditation practitioners, that blinds us to our True Will).

The term "King" or "Prince" usually refers to people of power or influence in the matter at hand; and these usually (but not always) also have good and virtuous qualities. Like the "Great Man", the "King" or "Prince" can refer to people of either gender; and when mentioned in reference to the caster, it is a reference to aspects of one's own being at higher levels of consciousness. Esoterically, the King is also a parallel to the "Celestial Emperor", that is, to the supreme Divine Force.

The Prince is thus representative of the subordinate force; in terms of qabalistic correspondences, these would be to Chokmah (the King) and Tiphareth (the Prince), respectively. There is also the term "Queen" or "Queen Mother", which is as above but would most usually refer to a female individual (or again, to the Divine Feminine Principle within one's self), corresponding to Binah on the Tree of Life. Likewise the "General" or "Commander" could be understood as corresponding to Yesod (as evidenced by the term being referred to frequently in connection to hexagrams where the Moon is one of the component trigrams), as representing the force of inspiration.

- **"Superiors"**: Anyone who would be in a position of authority over you, particularly regarding the question presented. The term "Lord" is essentially the same in this case.

- **"Virtue"**: At the basic level, this term refers to the core Confucian virtues of love, right conduct, justice, and wisdom, and the cultivation of the same. But these cannot be understood as mere ethics, feelings or attitudes, much less good manners. Virtue in this case is synonymous with "power"; that means that these are magical virtues, qualities that are cultivated because they increase the force of our Will, and thus grant us the ability to create change.

- **"Will"**: Your true inner will; this refers not to what you merely may want at any given time, but to your true sense of inner purpose. It is the force that connects your individual being to the Great Work. The Great Work itself is referred to as the "Will of Heaven".

- **"Women"**: there are several lines in the I Ching which suggest that a given oracle has different meanings depending on whether the person making the question is male or female. In some cases, the I Ching suggests that something is "good luck for women, bad luck for men"; in others it may say "right pushing is good for women". This generally implies that under the circumstances of the reading, the situation may be better for a woman than a man. However, the reason why this would be so must be considered: in the Chinese culture, what was "good luck" (or "bad luck") for women would have to do with matters related to the home, to stable relationships, and to the security brought about by social contracts. Thus if people, regardless of gender, would find themselves benefited by the conditions that the I Ching is describing that would create this good (or bad) luck, they should assume it applies to them.

In some cases, there are certain social activities (like gossip) that in Chinese culture was considered tolerable when practised by women (though still unbecoming) but that would be intolerable if practised by men. People in our society receiving a reading related to these sorts of activities will need to consider how it would apply to their situation based on the social conventions of our time. There is also an esoteric dimension to this meaning; "women" here is understood as the Yin quality, "men" as the Yang. So the idea of "women" in these verses can be taken esoterically to mean those who are energetically passive, receptive, yielding; while "men" are those who act with the Yang qualities of force and direct effort.

Reference Table for the Hexagrams

The table on the following page simplifies the process of looking up which section or chapter of the I Ching corresponds to the hexagram drawn from a reading. In the table, the top row corresponds to the trigram of three lines at the top places of your hexagram, while the left-hand row corresponds to the bottom trigram. The number on the table where the rows intersect is the number corresponding to the section of the I Ching where the resulting hexagram is found.

For example, if your I Ching reading generates three solid lines at the bottom (the "Heaven" trigram) and three broken lines at the top (the "World" trigram), the chapter of the I Ching where the hexagram formed by these lines can be found is Chapter Eleven.

General Notes on Interpreting A Reading

Rule 0: Look At What is Being Said, Don't Look For What You Want to Hear.

This is not just a rule for I Ching casting, it is the central rule for effective divination of any kind, and indeed for the cultivation of the "Superior Individual" (the True Will) in general. If you are projecting your own wishful thinking, instead of engaging in being receptive to the message presented, then all opportunity for change is lost. Transformation and harmony with one's Will, and the subsequent magical power this generates, comes from the steadfast determination to dare to face the Truth naked of adornment.

Reference Table for the Hexagrams

Top Trigram → / Bottom Trigram	Heaven	World	Sun	Moon	Fire	Water	Air	Earth
Heaven	1	11	14	5	34	43	9	26
World	12	2	35	8	16	45	20	23
Sun	13	36	30	63	55	49	37	22
Moon	6	7	64	29	40	47	59	4
Fire	25	24	21	3	51	17	42	27
Water	10	19	38	60	54	58	61	41
Air	44	46	50	48	32	28	57	18
Earth	33	15	56	39	62	31	53	52

Likewise, if someone tries to use the I Ching as a mere "answer machine", as a substitute for their own intuition rather than as an aid to the growth of their awareness and virtue (the cultivation of the "Superior Individual"), then what results from using it will be at best gibberish, and at worst one's own deceptive fantasies.

A Case Study on the Subject—The Fall of the Shang

In the era of the Shang dynasty, when the I Ching was already in use but not yet quantified into a book, the great Shang wizard-kings were expected to make regular auguries. At that time, the Shang used bones thrown in fire for their divination; specifically turtle shells and ox bones (the cracks the fire caused in the bone or shell would reveal the lines of Yin and Yang).

In the earlier Shang archaeological records, you see auguries about all sorts of subjects, and auguries where the King proclaimed good luck or bad: "we should attack this country", "if we attack now it will be disaster", "the king's second wife will have a child", "the queen will have a stillborn son". Prosperity and famine, bounty and disaster are both predicted.

However, by the later period of the Shang dynasty something interesting happens: the oracles the wizard-king declares become quite different, suddenly they are all very vague and generally good, one after another. There are thousands of declarations that say something like "the next period will be truly auspicious, with no misfortune".

The notable difference is that the earlier era was one where the Shang were the mightiest kingdom in their known world. The latter era, however, was one where the Shang had become corrupt: their last king was tyrannical toward his outlying provinces while engaging in decadent behaviour at home (legends hold that near the end he had built an artificial lake of wine with a paradisiacal island filled with deer meat at its centre, and sumptuous palaces where he held degenerate orgies that included the sadistic torture of commoners). Rival powers were emerging and the Shang dynasty would soon be overthrown, their kingdom over-run by the Zhou (including the great King Wen, who wrote the text of the I Ching and thus proved he had superior magical power and wisdom than the decadent kings of Shang).

It seems that in the earlier era, the people were willing to hear, and thus the king to declare, bad news as well as good. But in the latter era, when things had gone bad, the people didn't want to hear anything realistic from their government, they just wanted to keep being told everything was going to be great and there wouldn't be any problems; they wanted to be given reassuring lies. These oracles were the equivalent of "campaign promises" in modern elections; and by the end time of the Shang dynasty no ruler dared demand "blood, sweat or tears" from the people, or ask them to make sacrifices; instead he had to constantly repeat the story that everything was great, that they were the best country in the world, that every problem would be solved and no sacrifice would be needed. And of course, on the same note, the rulers were lying to themselves. Thus, the last Shang king was blinded by his own lesser nature, to the extent of executing wise counsellors who attempted to warn him of the dangers his kingdom faced.

This is what the Confucian commentaries of the I Ching would describe as the preponderance of the Inferior Person: a time of decadence that has spread to the moral, intellectual and vital faculties. At that point, only revolution (by the Zhou) could restore society. And indeed, King Wen's son fulfilled his father's dreams by uniting eleven of the border territories against the Shang, defeating their armies and conquering the kingdom. The last King of the Shang committed suicide on his deer meat island while his palaces burned.

In this little piece of I Ching history, there is a very interesting example of the kind of teaching the I Ching promulgates (and explanation of the context of the times in which the actual text of the I Ching was written). Likewise, it demonstrates the ways someone can use it effectively, or fail to apply it correctly. It is also an interesting message for our modern era, showing just how relevant the I Ching continues to be, 3,000+ years after the time of its writing, because the same problems keep happening.

The I Ching has, for thousands of years, warned us what happens to those individuals, as well as societies as a whole, who are fat and complacent, only wanting to hear "good oracles".

Further Guidelines

1. The structure of a hexagram is based on the combination of the two elemental trigrams, but the individual oracle is also based on the location of each line in the hexagram.

2. Generally speaking, a Yang (solid) line is well-placed if it is in an odd-numbered line (1,3,5), while a Yin (broken) line is well placed in an even-numbered line (2,4,6). The lines' significance is also affected by those lines around it: for example, a weak (Yin) line in the fifth place is generally bad, and a strong (Yang) line in the fourth place is generally undesirable; but if you have a Yin line in the fifth place surrounded (and thus "supported") by strong lines in 4 and 6, this improves the situation greatly. A weak (Yin) line in position 2 is going to be more auspicious if there is a strong (Yang) line in position 5 to mirror it. A weak (Yin) line in position 1 usually means that the hexagram's process is off to a bad start, it can't maintain the weight of the other lines; while a strong (Yang) line at the top (sixth) line often means things have been pushed too far.

3. Each line of a hexagram represents a development in the overall theme of the hexagram; thus the lines (from line 1 at the bottom to line 6 at the top) can be seen as marking an overall "timeline". If you have, for example, lines 4 and 6 as changing lines, you can usually assume that line 4 indicates an earlier development in the situation, and line 6 represents a later development.

4. The significance of each line in a hexagram is based on its position as well. Line 1 symbolizes the "lowest rank", the least important person, the outsider. Line 2 is the "common subject" (in the Confucian context, a "lowly official"); it is thus auspicious as a rule because the common subject has nothing to prove; where it is problematic is if it is left to its own devices without guidance. Line 3 is the "social climber", the person or situation in a state of transition; thus it usually means difficulties and challenges in order to achieve things. Line 4 is the "minister" line; someone in a position of important subservience; meant to assist the "ruler" of the fifth line. Line 5 is generally the "ruler"; it is often the most important line of the hexagram. When it isn't, it is a sign that the

hexagram represents a situation of disorder or instability; if the ruler is weak, or poorly supported, then problems are very likely. Line 6 represents the situation "after ending"; it is like an old retired man who has no place, or a situation that has gone on for too long or stretched too far. It can be positive only if things are overwhelmingly good overall, or if the line takes on the attitude of a "sage", removing itself voluntarily from the situation. There is one other situation where the sixth line can be positive: if the overall hexagram is relatively negative, then the last line often symbolizes an end to the bad situation and the first glimpse of positive changes.

5. It is particularly useful, when beginning to interpret the hexagram cast, to look at the component trigrams. These trigrams have a wealth of symbolism of their own (as already expressed above); and it is worthwhile to consider their significance separately and together in the hexagram. The "image" description in each hexagram text presents the traditional portrait of what the two hexagrams combined look like (e.g., hexagram #16, Certainty, composed of Fire above and World below, has the image of "signal fires lit over the world"), and this can often give great insight into the rest of the hexagram's meaning (the imagery of hexagram #16 connects to the idea of sending the signal because one is ready to march, hence it is related to the central text of this being "the time for sending out armies"; however these fires can also be an alarm, as per line 1 of the hexagram, or a sign that it is time to make offerings and sacrifices, as per the Confucian commentary).

6. Certainly, the image presented is only one possible way of considering the combination of elements. It can be a very worthwhile exercise to think of other possible images formed by the elements in combination, including images that come to mind as applicable to the question being asked.

7. Remember that "The I Ching is Not About You". An I Ching reading where you are using only your "active intellect", casting the staves or coins in an ordinary state of mind and then just reciting the text from the book and thinking hard about it, is likely to be a very sub-optimal reading. Just as with any system of divination, the I Ching's success depends on your ability to

"get out of your own way", to momentarily step out of ordinary consciousness into a light trance consciousness. In the case of the I Ching, it is a very light pattern of altered perceptions, so that you are engaging both mind and intuition together, in harmony (in keeping with the formula of Yi-Fa). When you first recite the lines of your casting, do so without trying to analyze: write them down, even if you already know them by heart, let yourself connect to them in a way that doesn't deconstruct them immediately. Then start looking carefully at each part of the casting and rather than forcing analysis, seek out insight.

8. Ask yourself what the words of the oracle mean in the context of your question. There is a famous story that Shao Yung was training his son in using the I Ching. One evening, a neighbour knocked on the family door and before their guest could explain his presence, Shao Yung told his son: "Quickly, consult the I Ching and guess from it what our neighbour wants". The younger man generated a hexagram and noted from only the image itself that it involved the combination of wood and metal, and declared to Shao Yung "Father, our visitor will ask to borrow a shovel!"

Shao Yung shook his head, "you are close, my son, but incorrect: he will ask for an axe." When they finally enquired, the neighbour had indeed come to borrow an axe. Shao Yung's son, surprised, asked him how he knew it was an axe and not a shovel. Shao Yung answered: "Because you observed the hexagram, but I observed both the hexagram and the nature that surrounds us: it is evening, and it is cold, and a man will not come looking for a shovel to dig for something when the sun is setting. But he may ask to borrow an axe to chop wood for a fire".

Make a point to observe nature, and to consider the application of the oracle to the environment that surrounds your question.

9. Finally, it will be essential for your development in the study of the I Ching that you study the text carefully. Read the descriptions of the hexagrams regularly, and consider their relationships to one another. In my experience, it makes a significant difference in one's ability to read the entire text through at least one time; and to regularly study the text and commentaries after that.

The other side of the equation to become a talented "Changeologist" is to keep track of the castings you perform, and verify whether your interpretations were accurate or not. It is important to be honest with yourself and with the results, to judge if the castings were on the mark, if the oracle itself was accurate but your interpretation flawed, or if the oracle did not appear to make sense. It is important to be able to study this over time; and the only sure way to accomplish this is to keep a record of all your castings, as well as notes on insights you receive from studying and contemplating the text. As such, I would very strongly urge that you keep a diary of your I Ching work, and be meticulous in recording your study and practice. This will lead to significant and swift progress.

Chapter Three

The Text of the I Ching

Outline

For each hexagram the information is presented in the following format:

a. Hexagram number, Chinese name (where appropriate with phonetic pronunciation), and English name.

b. Illustration of the hexagram.

c. List of the two trigram elements that constitute the hexagram.

d. A note on the hexagram's "Ruling and Governing Line(s)", if applicable. Each hexagram will have certain lines of particular importance, that are most central in the essence of the hexagram. These were traditionally called "ruling" or "governing" lines. The main difference being that the ruling lines tended to be lines that instructed on the central attitude of the individual, while the governing lines revealed the central nature of the situation.

While not applicable to divination as such, these can be most useful in the study and interpretation of the I Ching and are worthy of at least a couple of decades worth of contemplation to help understand the I Ching. Ruling or governing lines are also marked by a "*" (for ruling lines) or a "^" (for governing lines) in the line-description section.

e. A description of the Image evoked by the hexagram.

f. The Description of the main hexagram text.

g. Advice for what the Superior Individual is meant to do in the situation described by the hexagram to propitiate the Great Work.

h. A Commentary on the hexagram, based on the original Confucian commentary but rewritten for ease of study, with my own additional clarifications.

i. The Line descriptions. Remember that the lines are counted from *bottom to top*; thus "line 1" is the lowest line in the hexagram, while "line 6" is the top line.

A Note on Notes

You will find that there are several areas of blank spaces interspersed amidst the entries of the hexagrams. This is in order that the I Ching student may have room to write notes within the book itself. I strongly encourage the reader to do this if they wish to study the I Ching seriously.

I hope this book will not be left languishing on a shelf, untarnished by any markings, but rather that it will be used by serious students who will carry this book with them, and who will refer to it daily, going back and forth through its pages and taking notice of lines, words, imagery or comments that they had not noticed on previous readings. That they will get insights or ideas or questions about the I Ching text, and in the urge not to forget these insights will need to jot them down immediately! The spaces in the book will allow them to do so, close to the source material that inspired the insight in the first place.

And should it ever come up, I will only ever sign a well-worn copy with many mad scribblings between its pages...

The Core Text of the I Ching

Hexagram 1: Chien (pr. "chee-en")—Creation

Heaven and Heaven make Creation.

Image: Sublime Celestial Forces in Motion. (Note: in the original text these are literally four words: "Sublime", "Accomplishment", "Beneficence", "Determination"; Confucius notes that these are the four virtues of the Superior Individual: Love, Right Conduct, Justice, and Wisdom).

Ruling Line: 5

Description: Success! Pushing brings reward, if in a right course.

The Great Work: The Superior Individual must strengthen his development in the four virtues.

Commentary: The creative mind works through change. The Ruler, towering above the masses, brings peace to all peoples. Heaven and Heaven: clouds come forth, and bring rain at the right time for crops to grow and bring abundance. The imagery of this Hexagram is that of the Dragon, the supreme Creative power, choosing the right moment to come out of his cave. (The imagery of the Dragon in the I Ching is the pure masculine force, equivalent to the qabalistic Chokmah and the image of "Therion" or the "Great Beast")

The Six Lines of this first hexagram of the I Ching are archetypes; they summarize in the purest form the six phases of all Process of Change in the Universe.

The Lines:

1. The Dragon is hidden, avoid acting!
2. The Dragon comes out of his cave, it is time to seek the Superior Individual.

3. Keep busy all day, and watchful at night! There is danger—but harm is (thus) avoided.

4. The Dragon tries to jump high, he may fly over the abyss, or fall— no error! (The Superior Individual can accept either, without lust of result—this is a test, of one's ability to overcome limitations and persevere even facing failure, in order to grow).

5. * The Dragon Soars! He seeks the Superior Individual. (Clouds follow the dragon and bring good rains; to find the Great, be Great).

6. The proud Dragon will regret. (Because he reaches too far).

    If all the Dragons are changing, in motion, the Universe is blessed. (This means that if all six lines are changing, it is considered a particularly great augury).

Notes

Hexagram 2: Kun (pr. "kwn")—Passive

The World and The World are passive.

Image: Passive is all of The World.

Ruling Line: 2

Description: Passive is gentle success. The mare is a sign of good luck, peaceful and rightly pushing. If the Superior Individual has a goal, he may go wrong, but will find his way, with friends in the Southwest. Friends in the Northeast will be lost.

The Great Work: The Superior Individual embraces all!

Commentary: The Passive is an all-embracing vessel. If one pushes ahead roughly, he may be lost, it is good to have a guide. "Friends in the Southwest" means to seek friends among your own kind (from the context of the original writing, the southwest was civilized territory, while to the northeast were barbarians and enemies).

The Lines:

1. Frost on the ground means ice later.

2. * Straight and wide, prosperity comes without effort.

3. Hide talent and beauty: early failures, but victory in the end, assisting the King in the Great Work.

4. Stoic and quiet, prudent. No blame, no praise.

5. The (rich) golden robe brings gentle good luck.

6. Warring dragons spill black and yellow blood in the wilderness. The Passive way has come to an end. (black is the colour of Heaven, yellow of The World).

If all The World is changing, in motion, then do not give up: your Will shall be made constant. (This is again in reference to a good augury if all six lines are changing lines).

Notes

Hexagram 3: Chun (pr. "jwn")—Challenge

The Moon and Fire make challenge.

Image: Fire + Moon, lightning falls from the clouds at night.

Ruling Lines: 1 & 5.

Description: Challenge, then gentle success. Continue pushing your right path, do not look for new goals or locales. Consolidate things as they are.

The Great Work: The Superior Individual keeps busy getting things in order (while waiting out the storm).

Commentary: This hexagram marks the birth of the phenomenal world (as Fire is the first emanation of the four terrestrial or lower elements). Growth through a time of danger. The theme of the lines is of a difficult period of courtship and early wedded life.

The Lines:

1. * In chaos, better to stay still. Build up your Will. (the Yang at the bottom line subordinates himself to the three Yin that follow, to build up support).

2. Difficult beginnings; moving back and forth, no progress is made. The damsel plays "hard to get" for ten years! (the "damsel" is the Yin line).

3. Without a guide, the hunter loses his prey; if he persists, he will be disappointed. The Superior Individual knows to stay still.

4. Moving back and forth, waiting for marriage. When it comes, it will be prosperous. Be wise, seek favour.

5. * Troubles in conceiving; pushing for small things is good, but for large things, woe.

6. He runs around, back and forth, crying until he bleeds. What a drama queen!

Hexagram 4: Meng (pr. "mng")Immaturity

Earth and Moon are immature.

Image: A pit (Moon) at the foot of a mountain (Earth).

Ruling Lines: 2 & 5.

Description: When the immature seek out the wise, it will at first be helpful; but don't ask twice! No more explanation will he provide. Do not do more castings on this matter.

The Great Work: The Superior Individual must nourish his virtue, by being determined to be of right conduct.

Commentary: How one behaves at the start of things is very important. Receiving this hexagram can imply that you are consulting the oracle too frequently on this topic. The theme of the lines is of dealing with the folly of youth.

The Lines:

1. Correct and bind the youth to discipline, but also set a good example. If youth rushes forth without education, woe!

2. * Be gentle with the immature. Take a wife, have children. Good luck. Inheritance will come.

3. Don't choose a wife that lusts after rich or handsome men.

4. Stubborn immature fantasies cause harm and regret. He has strayed too far from the truths of his teacher! (This is because this Yin line is far away from the strong Yang lines).

5. * Pure youthful innocence will bring good luck, because he is receptive to his teacher's truth. (This is because this Yin line is close to a strong Yang line and the reflection of the strong Yang in line 2).

6. To deal with the immature, he tries to beat the child! To do what is right, he must instead show him that they are on the same side. The true enemy is ignorance, and you cannot fix a wrong with another wrong.

Notes

Hexagram 5: Hsu (pr. "shu")—Pause

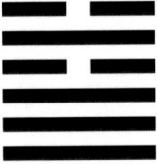

The Moon and Heaven unite to pause.

Image: The Moon at its peak; clouds gather in the sky.

Ruling Line: 5.

Description: Pause, and others' trust will bring shining success. Pushing rightly will bring luck. Cross the great river.

The Great Work: The Superior Individual should spend their time as in feasting and taking pleasure; waiting without concern for the appropriate opportunity to act.

Commentary: Do not be bewildered, do not rush forth. Do not be worried or seem insecure as you wait. Be firm. Waiting is to your advantage until the perfect moment arises.

The Lines:

1. Pause at the borderland. Be constant and you will be safe.

2. Pause at the shoreline. It will be scandalous, but lucky in the end.

3. Pause in the mud, and evil approaches. Don't get stuck, or you'll be hurt! Be discreet, and avoid brigands.

4. Pausing in a pool of blood, calm even in danger. Things will pass and you will escape from the pit. (This is in reference to being the weak lower line of the Moon trigram)

5. * Pause at the feast, entertain others with wine and food; but keep to the right path for gain.

6. He falls into the pit, danger! Three unexpected visitors arrive; showing hospitality to them brings good luck. (The pit is a reference to this being the weak top line of the Moon trigram).

Hexagram 6: Sung (pr. "soong")Struggling

Heaven and Moon unite in struggling.

Image: The Moon is low in the sky—an ill omen. Moon and Heaven are in the opposite of their natural places, this symbolizes dark times and conflicts.

Ruling Line: 5.

Description: When one's confidence and sincerity are doubted, a struggle commences. Care for justness and perseverance makes things work for a while, but the struggle pushed to its extreme would bring disaster. It is good if a Great Man comes and judges the dispute; but do not cross the river.

The Great Work: The Superior Individual does not engage in any activity without careful planning right from the beginning.

Commentary: The imagery of this hexagram is both of a needless or unjust war, and of a legal dispute. It begins because wickedness was not met by firmness right from the start. If the wicked think you lack conviction, conflict is inevitable (because they will take liberties).

The Lines:

1. Don't push the issue or speak too much; you will be slightly shamed, but will avoid starting a longer conflict. In the longer term, this is luckier. (This is in reference to the weak first line in the Moon trigram).

2. Overwhelmed, retreat; quickly! Take refuge with 300 family members. (This is in reference to the solid second line being surrounded by broken Yin lines; the "300 family members" are presaged by the three solid lines of the Heaven trigram).

3. Rely on ancient virtues, guard against dangers. Trouble at first, better later. Support the King but do not seek public office.

4. Overwhelmed, retreat, realize the folly (i.e., the unnatural mentality) of what you were thinking. Return to reason. Push for the right way, but seek peace (not revenge).

5. * Conflict ends with a fair judge arbitrating the dispute. Great fortune!

6. The sash of honour, given today, is lost tomorrow. Gained in strife, it brings little respect (because it was not truly deserved, for what was a needless conflict to begin with).

Notes

Hexagram 7: Shih (pr. "shrr")—The Army

The World and the Moon are an army.

Image: Water (in pits) deep beneath The World.

Ruling Line: 5.

Description: You must persevere on the right path. There is good luck and freedom from mistakes, if the chosen commander is wise.

The Great Work: The Superior Individual accepts and nourishes all who come to his side, and thus assembles an army.

Commentary: Persistence is needed to govern a large host. This is the quality of a King. The strong (the solid second line of the hexagram) must progress through difficult tasks and thus conquer, winning the people's allegiance.

The Lines:

1. Armies need discipline. If not, corruption and disaster follow! There must be discipline from the very start.

2. The general commands justly and has good fortune. He is honoured three times by the King, and given important offices!

3. An army of corpses: disaster on the battlefield, defeat!

4. The army retreats, and regroups in an orderly fashion: no mistake.

5. * Beasts in the field, but they are easy for the wise to spot. Choose the wise general and he leads the armies (to victory); choose an Inferior Person, and he will carry back corpses (in defeat).

6. The Prince takes command, all is well. He gives titles to the victorious generals. But an Inferior Person must not be given offices or disaster will follow.

Hexagram 8: Pi (pr. "bee")—Union

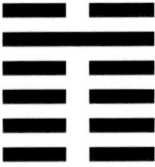

The Moon and The World are in union.

Image: The tides (from the Moon) naturally ebb and flow over The World.

Ruling Line: 5.

Description: Union! Luck. Vassals follow their Superior's Will. You must have a clear vision of the real situation. Anxious rebel Princes come back into union with the King. The lazy (those slow to answer the King's call) lag behind and face disaster. Do a second I Ching reading (on a related question) for great value.

The Great Work: The rulers of old did well by being on good terms with their vassals.

Commentary: Coordination works by bringing into the fold and assuring the support and loyalty of one's subordinates. The theme of this hexagram is uniting for common causes, or failing to do so.

The Lines:

1. Be confident and sincere. Assist the King, faultlessly. He will give you a windfall. Good fortune.

2. Unification of the inner circle (that is, of those in your close group). Right pushing is auspicious. (The "inner circle" refers to the united harmony of the weak second line with the strong fifth line)

3. Union with evil-doers brings suffering.

4. Union with the King is achieved even from those outside his inner circle (as the weak fourth line is in the outer edge of the Moon trigram); right pushing brings auspiciousness.

5. * The King loses his prey, but because he allows their escape. Thus he can see which traitors flee, and who remains loyal.

6. He hesitates too long to unite to the King's cause; he is forsaken and stands alone. Disaster!

Notes

Hexagram 9: Hsiao Chu (pr. "sheeau choo")—Small Nourisher

```
▬▬▬▬▬▬▬
▬▬▬▬▬▬▬
▬▬▬  ▬▬▬
▬▬▬▬▬▬▬
▬▬▬▬▬▬▬
▬▬▬▬▬▬▬
```

Air and Heaven make small nourishment.

Image: The wind (Air) blows softly across the sky (Heaven). Dense clouds form but there is not yet rain (this is in reference to the broken line at number 4, which is still in the process of rising).

Ruling Line: 5.

Governing Line: 4.

Description: Small nourishment, promising. Success. Dense clouds form in the western borderlands, but there is no rain yet.

The Great Work: The Superior Individual should engage in scholarly matters (a reference to the Air element), and refine his virtue (a reference to the Heaven element).

Commentary: The "west" implies that problems could arise from unstable territories, but these have not yet manifested. Our affairs can thus continue (in the early lines of this hexagram, the implication is that one should not stop what one is doing out of concern yet). The theme of this hexagram's lines simultaneously describe (in literal terms) the build-up of bad weather in the distance, and (in allegorical terms) potential unrest in the border territories of a Kingdom.

The Lines:

1. Come back to this path, there is no harm, and good luck (in continuing).

2. Bringing yourself back to the right way, returning to your duties and commitments, good luck!

3. The wheel of the carriage breaks; husband and wife quarrel and separate.

4. ^ Fear and struggle are avoided by confident support. (Implied by the strong fifth line protecting the weak fourth line)

5. * Confidence leads the strong to unite to you, and you can thus be benevolent to troubled neighbours.

6. The clouds build up too much, they cannot contain themselves. Rain pours down. The moon has become full and now there is danger (particularly for women). If the Superior Individual keeps trying to build himself up, there will be disaster.

Notes

Hexagram 10: Lu—Stepping

Heaven and Water unite in stepping.

Image: Water flows openly downstream, accessible to all.

Ruling Line: 5.

Governing Line: 3.

Description: He walks carefully, following the tiger, but is not bitten. Success!

The Great Work: The Superior Individual communicates with the high and the low alike, steadying the people's will, and directing them back to the proper rites.

Commentary: The tiger represents Heaven's force. The strong (Heaven) is above, and the joyful (Water) is below. The tiger walks and one moves behind it, following its firm trail. The tiger follows its Will, and the wise man does likewise. As a ruler governs with strength and virtue (and people follow him joyously), so should you set foot blamelessly (that is, with full consciousness) in the place of the Supreme Ruler, for glory. The theme of the lines is of following the Tiger while trying not to step on its tail.

The Lines:

1. Be simple and straightforward, perform the proper rites. Then you advance without blame.

2. Hermits walk peacefully along the trail. Right pushing brings luck. Without hesitating, he knows the path, having performed ancient rites.

3. ^ A blind man tries to see, a cripple tries to walk; step on a tiger's tail and get bitten! Disaster! Subsume your will to the King's will!

(The blind try to see, without awareness; the crippled try to move, without ability.)

4. Stepping on a tiger's tail, pause and don't even breathe! Fear. Use caution, and the tiger will not bite; good luck follows.

5. * Step softly, but with determination. Trouble is nearby, but acting properly will avoid it.

6. Watching your steps, remembering, heeding the signs; note the difference between fortune and disaster. Know when to stop and when to turn back; you will thus receive a great blessing.

Notes

Hexagram 11: Tai—Harmony/Intercourse

The World and Heaven unite in harmony.

Image: Male and Female (Heaven and The World) in intercourse with each other. Note that the female is above the male (an allusion to a technique present in Taoist Sexual Alchemy, Tantra, and other schools of Sexual Magick). This hexagram is a symbol equivalent to the western magical symbol of the Holy Hexagram.

Ruling Lines: 2 and 5.

Description: Harmony. All is as it should be. The Base decline, and the Great and Good enters. Good luck, and success.

The Great Work: The Superior Individual penetrates to the heart of all things, for the sake of the Great Work.

Commentary: The high and the low are of one Will. Strength (Heaven) is inside, while softness (The World) is yielding and lustful. There may be a historical significance to the line-descriptions of this hexagram; they appear to tell the story of the period of harmony between the Shang and the Zhou, when King Wen's father maintained his loyalty to the Shang King in spite of mounting unrest. The Shang King married one of his daughters to the ruling family of Zhou, and thus maintained stability for one more generation through their mutual good will. As presaged by the sixth line, eventually decadence set in and inevitably the period of harmony came to an end.

The Lines:

1. Pull up grass and you get its roots. It is good to go ahead with plans, progress will be swifter than expected.

2. * If your vision is vast, you can cross rivers even without boats. Do not forget your friends, even when far away. Avoid having

your own agenda, and instead serve the King, staying centred (on the Great Work).

3.   The steep follows the flat; don't lose heart, persist! No error. Even if others doubt you at first, fulfil your public office.

4.   Always ready to serve, he stays loyal in his modest place. His friends (thus) do likewise. ("Friends" refers to the fifth and sixth lines).

5.   * The old King's youngest daughter is given for marriage. Happiness and good luck; blessings come due to impartiality. (the King, referred to by name in this line, was the second-last King of the Shang Dynasty; according to historical legend he may have married his daughter to King Wen's father as a show of impartiality, which maintained peace for one more generation between the Shang and the Zhou).

6.   The city walls are crumbling; this is no time to go off to war! Keep order; cut through red tape and guard against chaos. Though this is right, you will likely face criticism. Harmony is decaying into decadence and stuckness.

Notes

Hexagram 12: Pi (pr. "pee")—Stuckness

Heaven and The World unite in stuckness.

Image: Male and Female do not meet in intercourse.

Ruling Line: 5.

Governing Line: 2.

Description: Stuckness due to the wicked. Nothing is beneficial. A bad omen, but the Superior Individual must keep pushing rightly. The Great and Good decline, the Base rise up (filling and blocking all opportunities for growth).

The Great Work: The Superior Individual should withdraw and look within, declining all temptations of superficial honours or riches. Be thrifty, and avoid danger.

Commentary: Everything is out of intercourse with everything else. The Yin is within, and Yang is without. The King and his subjects do not communicate. Weakness at the centre; mean men govern there, while the strong and honourable are exiled to the fringes.

The Lines:

1. Pull up grass, and you get its roots. Right pushing brings good luck and success. Stay loyal, keep persevering for the sake of the King.

2. ^ Criminals flatter great men, their crimes are pardoned and they rise up (to undeserved offices). The Superior Individual seeks no favours, flattery, or pardon for doing his Will. Nor does he deviate due to the decadence that surrounds him.

3. The pardoned criminal continues his corruption. He hides his blame but causes great shame in the end.

4. He brings reforms in accordance with the law (Heaven), and cannot go wrong. His companions (his comrades in the cause) are likewise honoured and blessed.

5. * Even in stuckness the Superior Individual can find fortune. He must remind himself constantly to avoid corruption.

6. The time for reform has come; at first some stuckness persists, but the corrupt is gradually removed. Then great joy follows.

Notes

Hexagram 13: Tong Ren (pr. "toong rn")—Fellowship

Heaven and the Sun make lovers and friends.

Image: Heaven and the Sun are natural brothers in their closeness.

Ruling Lines: 2 and 5.

Description: Finding fellowship, even in distant barbarian lands—success! Establish fellowship. Cross great rivers. The Superior Individual benefits if he keeps pushing rightly.

The Great Work: The Superior Individual treats others as he would himself. He finds similarities and cause for brotherhood even among foreigners.

Commentary: Someone weak occupies the central position (broken line 2) but responds well to the creative force (solid line 5). This is the refining influence. It is the pure Virtue of the Superior Individual that lets them find brotherhood in others. Eventually the strong (the five solid lines) will integrate the weak (line 2). The theme of the lines involves reaching out to a barbarian tribe, making peace with them, and integrating them into the Kingdom.

The Lines:

1. Fellowship in your own neighbourhood, no harm in that.

2. * Fellowship within one's own tribe—trouble! Disappointing, no growth. (Having a sense of fellowship only among your own group is limiting).

3. They planned an ambush, but then ran for the hills! They dare not attack for three years. (They fear the strength of the opposing force).

4. They besiege the city walls but then pull back (a ceasefire is declared)—good luck!

5. * Trying to establish fellowship with a foreigner (the weak second line). There is weeping and shouting at first, but laughter in the end. Joining forces, they win a great battle, and others come to their side.

6. He looks for fellowship in lonely frontier regions; no fellowship is found, but there is no blame (in trying).

Notes

Hexagram 14: Ta Yu (pr "da you")—Great Holdings

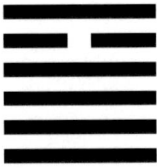

The Sun and Heaven make great holdings.

Image: The Sun is high in the Heavens, the Sun in splendour.

Ruling Line: 5.

Description: He who has much—great success! Riches and virtue.

The Great Work: The Superior Individual suppresses the evil and upholds the virtuous. He promotes charity, and obeys Heaven's orders. Most are on his side.

Commentary: Because he has splendour (Sun) and vigour (Heaven), he causes the strong to agree to his Will. Being responsive to Heaven, and doing things at the right time, success is won.

The Lines:

1. Do not mingle with others, stay away from the wrong. If you are not involved, there is no blame, even in trouble. Consider potential pitfalls to avoid harm.

2. The (merchant) wagons are full and ready to leave for their destination. If you have a goal, leaving now you cannot fail.

3.   A Duke can afford to pay the King's price, but an Inferior Person would ruin himself if he tried.

4. He is wealthy but modest, humble in success—no error.

5. * In society he is sincere and confident, earning respect. Dignity is the greatest wealth. Good fortune! (He is poor, but rich in dignity, honest and bold in demeanour, and thus wins great regard).

6. Blessings. Protected by Heaven, good luck and success in all endeavours.

Hexagram 15: Qian (pr. "chee-en")—Humility

The World and Earth are humble.

Image: A mountain in the centre of a flat plain: too much of things in one place, not enough in others.

Ruling Line: 3.

Description: Humility brings success. The Superior Individual acts with humility and thus takes things from beginning to end.

The Great Work: The Superior Individual weighs and balances things equitably, apportioning from the large to the small.

Commentary: Change tends to diminish the full and augment the humble, or help to maintain it. Human nature loathes the high, but loves the humble. No one can manage to up-end the humble.

The Lines:

1. The Superior Individual, with humility and discipline, will ford the great river—good luck.

2. His humility is heard in others' hearts. Right pushing brings good luck.

3. * The Superior Individual is hardworking and humble, bears fruits in his efforts, and remains humble even at the end—good luck.

4. Auspiciousness to those whose humility is nurtured and sincerely displayed.

5. Be modest and charitable about your wealth. Thus looked upon favourably by neighbours, they unite to your cause attacking outlaws. Everything in the expedition goes in your favour.

6. Your fame of humility is known far and wide. The call comes
   to command the armies, marching now to pacify neighbouring
   countries for the King and the good. (Your humility works against
   you in that it makes you notable for obligatory duties)

Notes

Hexagram 16: Yu—Certainty

Fire and The World unite in certainty.

Image: Signal fires lit across the land.

Ruling Line: 4.

Description: Certainty benefits those who build empires, apportion vassal states, and send out armies!

The Great Work: Ancient rulers made solemn music to venerate the Virtue of Heaven, and sacrificed to the Celestial Lord and to the honour of ancestors.

Commentary: Anything willed can be done. Action in accordance to the Will brings certainty. Certainty moves in accord with Nature. Thus all things move without error. This is a time of great significance, and timely application (of the hexagram) is vital!

The Lines:

1. The men took pleasure in indulgence last night, and are too long getting ready at the sound of the alarm—(potential) disaster.

2. Certain as a rock, appropriate (in moderation) with pleasures, right pushing will bring good luck before the day's end.

3. Flattering his superiors for his own gratification, this brings regret if not corrected quickly. More regrets (if correction is delayed).

4. * Great results from certainty; have no doubt. He pleases others, befriending officials, and gains much. His friends stay close to his side.

5. Illness foretold, but careful attention avoids danger. He will retain his health and not die.

6. Crazy indulgence! Confusion. Only timely change of ways can prevent harm.

Hexagram 17: Sui (pr. "sway")—Following

Water and Fire unite in following.

Image: Thunder rumbling in a lake.

Ruling Lines: 1 and 5.

Description: Following. Great success. Right pushing brings gain, and no mistake or harm.

The Great Work: Noting the times, seeing darkness fall, the Superior Individual goes inside (his home) and rests, knowing there is no more to be done.

Commentary: The firm (Fire) below follows the soft (Water); movement and joy conjoined. All the Universe is in accord with what Time dictates for it. Move in accord with the pulse of Time! Acting at the appropriate moment is vital.

The Lines:

1. * Ideas change over time. The powerful must also change. Rightly pushing your Will brings good luck. Leave home and mingle with outsiders. Results follow.

2. Following the Inferior Person, he loses the Superior Individual. Following fashion, he loses what worked. You cannot follow two ways at once.

3. Following the Superior Individual, he loses the Inferior Person. Following the old, he loses the fashionable, but gains what is sought. Make no move, be steadfast and determined in your Will.

4. Following a deceiver brings disaster. But if you are true, no harm comes. Being open and honest, others will follow you and all benefit.

5. * Treating all good people with sincerity, certainty in following. Good luck!

6. Captured, he is forced to follow. He is put in irons! The King must go do penance and sacrifice on mountaintops.

Notes

Hexagram 18: Ku (pr. "goo")—Repair

Earth and Air unite in repairing.

Image: Wind blows down the foot of a mountain.

Ruling Line: 5.

Description: What has decayed now begins to be repaired. Gentle success. Cross the great river. What came before will come again; look carefully at what took place three days before, you can then predict what will have to be done for the next three days.

The Great Work: The Superior Individual stimulates hearts, and nourishes the people's Virtue.

Commentary: When people are receptive, decay can be rectified. Only hard work going forward can bring opportunities. Heaven's activity is such that all endings are followed by new beginnings.

(The theme of this hexagram may refer to ritual exorcism to atone for parental errors; it may also be in reference to King Wen's son completing his father's wish in rebelling against the corrupt Shang monarchs)

The Lines:

1. Children fix the errors of their fathers. The dead are exorcised of blame, evil is repaired. Sons can complete their father's work. Luck in spite of danger.

2. Children fix the errors of their mother. Though difficult, push rightly and wait for the right opportunity.

3. Taking responsibility for a father's errors may bring regret, but no blame or harm.

4. Failing to resolve your father's errors will eventually cause regret. (It will be harder to repair the longer you put it off)

5. * Taking responsibility for your father's errors, by Virtue you will win honour and praise.

6. Serve your Will, more than any king or prince's commands.

Notes

Hexagram 19: Lin—Convergence (of Will)

The World and Water are converging.

Image: An island on a lake.

Ruling Lines: 1 and 2.

Description: Convergence of Will (between superiors and their subjects). Great success! Right pushing brings gain, but in the eighth month, force declines and misfortune begins.

The Great Work: The Superior Individual's teaching and affection for his subordinates is inexhaustible. He gives his all to nurture and enlighten his people.

Commentary: Great success is won by individuals obeying their superior's Will, and directing their subordinates; thus are all things rectified. But this will soon wane, as the initial Will has trouble being maintained (this is due to the solid lines being used up too early in the hexagram).

The overall theme of the lines involves the convergence of the Will throughout different levels; between ruler and minister, between minister and subject.

(There is a mystical symbolism in this, of connecting one's consciousness to the True Will, and in turn directing those lower forces; invoking the Holy Guardian Angel, uniting that true Will to the Will of the Universe, while in turn evoking lesser forces; Goetic spirits, for example).

The Lines:

1. * His Will converges with his superior (the True Will). Right pushing brings gain.

2. * All converges—he does the will of the King! Good luck; and all problems are thus far still only illusory.

3. He flatters his inferiors; no true benefit can be gained (from this attitude). He gets nowhere, talking much and doing little. But if he pays attention, and doesn't settle for this, it is not too late to correct errors.

4. He closely supervises his inferiors, benevolent toward them but not flattering. Perfect convergence—no mistake.

5. Wise convergence, he invokes the nature of the King in his Virtue —good luck!

6. He is magnanimous, putting aside his own ambitions to serve the Kingdom. Honest and sincere, he supervises his inferiors with certainty. Good luck and no error.

Notes

Hexagram 20: Kwan (pr. "gwan")—Contemplating

Air and The World unite in contemplating.

Image: Wind blows over the land.

Ruling Lines: 5 and 6.

Description: Contemplating. The rite of communion being mastered, you may bypass the technical details of the sacrifice, because you are filled with the essence of Heaven's Virtue.

The Great Work: Rulers of old visited many regions, to observe and learn rites, and in turn they instructed the people.

Commentary: Contemplating means being able to observe the vast picture from a high place. Because the Sage has become receptive to Nature's Virtue, he is respected by all. If one cannot embody Heaven yet, he must follow the technical disciplines meticulously in his rites. He who attains to the Heavenly essence may now give instructions in any land. (The mystical symbolism of this hexagram relates to the type of awareness gained through powerful shifts in perspective. In western terminology, this would be the Knowledge & Conversation of the Holy Guardian Angel; one who gains this degree of Adept-hood is able to understand the essence and not just the technique, only then does he have the freedom to modify the rituals. In general it refers to the difference between investigation that is mere curiosity, or technical trivia, and actual comprehension. Aleister Crowley was on record saying that this hexagram related to the secrets of sexual alchemy, the "rites of communion" being its technique.)

The Lines:

1. Contemplating childishly (trivially, without deeper understanding) is to be expected and may even be a necessary step for the Inferior Person, but will be unsatisfying and disappointing to the Superior Individual.

2. Spying through keyholes is advantageous to women (though shameful!).

3. Contemplate Virtue, and judge yourself by that standard; then you will know whether to go forth, or retreat.

4. Contemplate the many different regions of the Kingdom (observing and learning); and then you will become the honoured guest of the King!

5. * He is viewed with great respect by the people, and yet he does not stop examining himself critically. (This is virtuous.)

6. * There is no wrong in being admired for your Virtue and conduct. Nor is it wrong to ceaselessly continue in your cultivation regardless.

Notes

Hexagram 21: Shih Ho (pr. "shrr heh")—Chewing

Sun and Fire make chewing.

Image: Sun and heat, thunder and lightning.

Ruling Line: 5.

Description: Chewing. Success! A good time for legal processes, and bringing criminals to justice.

The Great Work: Rulers made Law clear to all, and then enforced it solemnly and vigorously.

Commentary: Something is held between the jaws (an allusion to the shape of the hexagram: line 4 is the "something", held between the "jaws" of lines 1 and 6). The weak (line 5) is contained by the strong (lines 4 and 6). Thus this is a good time for the application of Law (material, or spiritual). The theme is of chewing (i.e., working through something, the process of dissolving something difficult).

(The mystical interpretation here is of using the Law of Heaven to establish discipline and to "punish", adjust or reform the "criminal" elements of the Inferior Person.)

The Lines:

1. The criminal's feet are shackled, he cannot walk. No error in this! The just application of discipline avoids recidivism.

2. Chewing into the soft outer layer, things go smoothly without difficulty. The criminal's nose is cut off—no error! (because he then submits to proper conduct).

3. Chewing dry meat, he is poisoned, failing (through this indigestion) to carry out his disciplines. Disappointment, but no long term harm. (He has used out-dated methods).

4. Chewing tough gristly meat, discipline is not carried out well. But he is firm and determined like a golden arrow (i.e., his inner Will is strong). There is much opposition, your discipline is not well-looked upon by others; but stay strong in difficulty—luck.

5. * Chewing dry meat, discipline is not carried out well; but he is steady in temperament, solid and golden (i.e., his inner Will is now firmly established). Be determined to guard against danger. There is trouble, but no error.

6. The stupid criminal is put in stocks, and his ears are cut off—woe! He is too stubborn to mend his ways. Distrust your predilections.

Notes

Hexagram 22: Pi (pr. "bee")—Adornment

Earth and Sun unite in Adornment.

Image: Sunlight bathes the foot of a mountain. That is, it is beautiful but will not be seen for very long.

Ruling Lines: 2 and 6.

Description: Adornment. Success. It is right for those in a position of weakness (or smallness) to have goals.

The Great Work: The Superior Individual is open and elegant, but not frivolous or too lenient in his judgements.

Commentary: Reaching only a certain level of growth, and then stopping, is the pattern of the common man. Refinement and ritual are the great advancements of human civilization. By contemplating the nature of Reality, studying human capacity, and seeing the pattern of Time unfolding, we can change ourselves, our environment, and The World.

The Lines:

1. Having properly adorned his feet, he can leave his carriage and walk for himself on solid ground. He does not have to rely on others to move.

2. * Adorn the beard (i.e., support the Will) of your Superior (as line 2 supports line 3).

3. His adornments shine—following the right Will to the very end brings luck, and mutual benefit for his supporters.

4. Adorned in white, on a white horse; the suitor is looked upon with suspicion (some think him a bandit). But if he goes forward, in spite of the doubts of others and even of his own, he will be satisfied in the end.

5. He (the Master) humbly tends to and adorns his modest garden. All he can offer his virtuous subordinate is a poor and simple belt (i.e., a discipline) as a gift. Those below him may decide not to respond to his offer of work; disappointing! But if those above him take notice, there will be luck, and happiness in the end!

6. * In an exalted position, he can adorn himself plainly (with nothing to prove). No error.

Notes

Hexagram 23: Po (pr. "poh")—Shedding

Earth and The World are shedding.

Image: A landslide from a mountain-top, down to a valley.

Ruling Line: 6.

Description: Shedding. No goal or destination can be worthy now.

The Great Work: The Great, in high positions, must reorganize their lifestyles to avoid collapse. They can show generosity to those under them who are virtuous (while shedding themselves of those who are not).

Commentary: The Inferior Person becomes powerful and affects the strong. Stay where you are and accept the situation (but seek reform). The Superior Individual contemplates the ebb and flow of all things. The shedding of hindrances is advised, progressively (through the lines), getting rid of things and people we relied upon (because they cannot be trusted). This will lead to growth in the long run, through the gradual shedding off of obstacles.

The Lines:

1. The foot of the bed is damaged (corruption at the very bottom). He sheds subordinates finding no firm foundations (of trust). Only right determination avoids disaster.

2. The head of the bed is also damaged. No loyalty is found (among friends or those intimate with you). Only right determination in shedding avoids disaster!

3. Shed off all that is above and all below alike—error is thus avoided.

4. The very mattress of his bed must be shed—disaster! (Everything must be thrown out.)

5. The palace maids are all in order and wait to be given favours from the King. No blame, in spite of troubles.

6. * Only the richest fruit remains available to be plucked. If the Superior Individual gains it, he can ride forth in his carriage, and give protection and happiness to the people. If the Inferior Person gets it first, his uselessness will ruin the households of thousands!

Notes

Hexagram 24: Fu (pr. "foo")—Return

The World and Fire unite in returning.

Image: Fire, deep below The World.

Ruling Line: 1.

Description: Return! Success. When strength (the strong first line) returns, whether from without or from within, there is no error. All things follow their cycle in nature, and in seven days the strong will return. It will (then) be safe to come or go, and good to have a goal. Adventurous friends gather together!

The Great Work: Wise Kings of old forbade activity or travel on Holy Days. They regimented themselves likewise (by the same rule).

Commentary: The strong (solid line at the bottom) has returned. The strong (Yang) is only starting to return and grow in power, from the base of the hexagram. Strength returns so only now can we come to understand how things we thought bad or unlucky served their purpose (in ultimately bringing about renewal). The theme is of returning to a strong and healthy way, after reactions to chaos lead one astray.

The Lines:

1. * Returning from close-by, before having gone too far. Trouble is thus avoided. Some regret, but swift correction to the right ways brings good luck.

2. Return blessed by heaven—good luck comes from treating others (who are below you) kindly.

3. Reluctantly forced to return. There's trouble, but if you return in the right way then harm is avoided.

4. Halfway along, he is forced to return alone (to avoid being led astray by others).

5. Returning for a good cause, honest and sincere, brings no regrets. Examine yourself.

6. Confused, lost, he doesn't know how to return. Bad luck. Disaster and harm. In command of troops, his army is crushingly defeated. In public office, the minister misrules and brings on ten years of chaos!

Notes

Hexagram 25: Wu Wang (pr. "woo wang")—Integrity and Fortune

Heaven and Fire make integrity.

Image: A chance firestorm rolls across The World. This gives energy for new growth, to those who respect and stand in awe of creation.

Ruling Lines: 1 and 5.

Description: Integrity. Great success. Right pushing brings reward; failing to follow the Will leads to disaster. Avoid having a firm goal or destination.

The Great Work: Rulers studied the course of changes in nature, and used their Virtue to help things and people grow.

Commentary: Fire is movement, Heaven is strength. A strong line (at the bottom) enters from without, and becomes chief within. Firmness finds resonance with the weak second line. Be mindful of the power of Heaven, you cannot control it. If you try to force your own way (instead of following the Will), then you will face disaster! There's no going anywhere without the invocation of the Will of Heaven above you. Do what is right (your true Will) to gain success.

One important element of the line readings of this hexagram is that integrity is a value in and of itself, life does not inherently reward those with integrity; disasters can still happen to those with integrity. However, integrity rewards itself, and changes how we deal with disaster.

The Lines:

1. * He moves forward with integrity, advancing brings good luck!

2. He doesn't plant or plow the fields, how can he expect a profitable harvest? It is good to have a goal.

3. Unexpected calamity! (it can befall even those with integrity) The wanderer finds an ox, the farmer lost an ox. Be careful about who you blame for problems.

4. Right pushing is essential now, to avoid harm in the long-term.

5. * Unexpected illness, it can strike those with integrity as well! But it is best not to panic (foolishly thinking that illness is somehow not part of nature too) and try to treat it carelessly with untested medicine. (Don't look for "miracle cures").

6. Even with integrity, if he acts at the wrong time he invites disaster. It is better not to go anywhere.

Notes

Hexagram 26: Ta Chu (pr. "dah choo")—The Great Nourisher

Earth and Heaven unite in great nourishment.

Image: A mountaintop rises above the clouds.

Ruling lines: 5 and 6.

Description: The Great Nourisher smiles on right pushing. Do not stay home, go, gather with others and eat at the court of the King. Cross the great river.

The Great Work: The Superior Individual studies the words and acts of the ancient Sages to gain their power of Virtue.

Commentary: Firmness, strength, and daily growth of Virtue is called for. The firm (sixth line) ascends and pays respect to the worthy. Discipline in the use of the Will is the excellent way! Follow the Will of Heaven.

The Lines:

1. Danger, threat! Cease all advance. Do not even try to oppose troubles at this time (or you'll only invite more trouble).

2. The cart's axle breaks, and you must halt. No blame.

3. A fast horse! Enduring through hardships, master your horse and defend yourself from opposition. But do not stop advancing!

4. Yoke the young ox, teach it discipline. Happiness and luck follow.

5. * Geld the boar and blunt its tusks. Preventing trouble is cause for celebration, and brings good luck.

6. * Following Heaven's ways, Virtue makes the road wide and smooth. (Discovering your Will creates a vast perspective that allows unfettered movement.)

Hexagram 27: Yee—Eating

Earth and Fire unite in eating.

Image: Fiery change at the foot of a mountain.

Ruling Lines: 5 and 6.

Description: Eating. Right pushing for good luck. Watch how people (try to) feed themselves, and how they think to feed others. From this understand how to best feed yourself.

The Great Work: The Superior Individual is thoughtful in speech, and frugal in eating and drinking.

Commentary: Nourish yourself on what is fitting. Heaven and The World give nourishment to all. Find food for yourself by the right ways (that is, find the right nourishment). The Sage nourishes both the virtuous and the unworthy alike, even if they do not understand or appreciate him. The theme of "eating" is about a disciple seeking Truth.

The Lines:

1. He wants to fancy himself like a magical being who can live without eating. He abandons his search (for food), but still drools when seeing others eating. Woe! (his notions are worthless).

2. He leaves the fertile valley (line 1) and seeks to abandon society for the broken hilltops, looking to be fed by hermits. Persisting in this course is disaster.

3. He tries to be fed by some outlandish method (that is, some odd teaching). Trying this for ten years, he proves to be useless the entire time. His methods are pointless and perverse.

4. Eating on the mountaintop; enlightened and sharing with others. Good luck. His glare is like a tiger's! (Through Will he has found something of substance.)

5.   * Normal ways have been abandoned. Right enduring will bring luck to those who stay still. Don't cross the river.

6.   * Eating brings trouble, many depend on him. Guard against dangers, good luck! Cross the Great River, and you will be blessed.

Notes

Hexagram 28: Ta Kuo (pr. "da gwo")—Excess (weight)

Water and Air unite in excess.

Image: A forest (Air) has been drowned by a flood (Water).

Ruling Lines: 2 and 4.

Description: The beam sags, it cannot hold. It is good to have a goal or path. Success!

The Great Work: The Superior Individual, although alone, is free from fear. He has no trouble withdrawing from the world.

Commentary: Too much weight (the solid Yang lines) in the middle, while the outer (first and sixth lines) are weak. The second line is unsuitably placed. Moving quickly (and thus avoiding the weak spot when you are strong) can free you from trouble, but timely application is vital. The theme is of a beam or tree trying to hold up great weight (the environment is unable to handle the growth of strength).

The Lines:

1. With gentle care, he uses reeds to make humble mats to present to the elder. No error—do things as well as you can with what you have.

2. * The old tree grows new branches. The old man can marry the young girl. All can be favourable.

3. The beam sags, not being well supported. Disaster!

4. * The beam gets propped up, blame is avoided. If it starts sagging (from having more weight put on it) there will be bad luck.

5. The old tree blossoms. The old woman marries a boy; not good, not bad, just embarrassing.

6. Crossing the river, he drowns in the deep water. His death came at the time appointed by nature, and led to greater good. Thus there is bad luck, but no blame.

Notes

Hexagram 29: Kan (pr. "cun")—The Pit/ Abyss

Moon and Moon are a pit.

Image: Abyss within Abyss! A deep pit filled with water.

Ruling Lines: 2 and 5.

Description: The pit—danger upon danger! Discipline your consciousness; honesty and openness will allow one to be magnanimous (in trouble). Struggling to endure unto the end will win respect.

The Great Work: The Superior Individual holds to unwavering Virtue, and spends much time trying to teach others the same.

Commentary: Great danger, but going with the flow he may traverse the Abyss without loss of certainty. Holding firm in his Will (with the strong lines in 2 and 5) lets him see it through. Nothing escapes dangers from Heaven, but worldly dangers are no more than mountains, hills, and great rivers. Princes set up border walls at dangerous places to defend the nation; Kings engaged in dangerous intrigues to protect the realm. What wonders can be done in times of danger! Timely application of the hexagram is essential. (Being double Moon, this hexagram refers to the profound unconscious; it can thus be related to the idea of the Abyss in western magick, and the power of dispersion of the forces that rule the Abyss. The theme of the lines involve awareness serving as a means to avoid falling into a pit.)

The Lines:

1. Pit upon pit! He fails to be cautious, falls in, and is lost—disaster!

2. * Danger in the pit. You can gain ground by solving smaller problems, but you are still trapped in a pit.

3. Grave danger near the pit of pits. Going forward is risky, but going back will leave you unable to live with yourself. If you fall into an Abyss, you will be completely unable to help your self.

4. A bucket of wine and rice is lowered through the cell window into the prison-pit. Staying true to the imprisoned elder, friendship brings no blame at the very end.

5. * The pit has not yet filled with water, and a rescue is planned. Danger still persists, but no harm done yet (and hope is not lost).

6. Bound with black rope and imprisoned in a pit surrounded by thorns. For three years you will fail to gain anything, making grandiose plans without first obtaining your freedom.

Notes

Hexagram 30: Li (pr. "lee")—Flaming Majesty

Sun and Sun make flaming majesty.

Image: The rising Sun emanates a double beam of burning light.

Ruling Lines: 2 and 5.

Description: Flaming majesty. Right pushing gains. Success! Caring for gentle livestock—good luck!

The Great Work: The Superior Individual perpetuates the light of Truth, to benefit and illuminate every quarter under Heaven.

Commentary: The Sun and Moon depend upon the power of Heaven. Plants depend upon The World. If we are clear on what is Natural, we can transform the world. The weak (the broken lines at 2 and 5) are properly cared for by the strong (the solid lines around them).

(The theme of the lines is of manifesting the Solar force).

The Lines:

1. Approach things seriously, respectfully, pay reverence, and keep silence. No Error.

2. * Golden sunlight—gentle good luck. Follow the middle way.

3. Sunset. If the young man stays quiet now (and does not make joyous noise), then the old man will sigh later. Bad luck, majesty fades. (Bad luck if you fail to seize the moment).

4. Sunrise brings beams of flaming light! Then it fades away fast. (It comes quickly and is lost quickly, a beautiful illusion).

5. * Tears and heavy sighs, but his distress is noticed and the Ruler aids him—good luck! (He is noted in his distress because he is a central position, in line 5).

6. The King is blessed. He goes forth to war and crushes the rebel leaders, taking many prisoners with little bloodshed.

Notes

Hexagram 31: Hsien (pr. "shee-en")—Feelings (Sensation)

Water and Earth are feelings.

Image: A mountain-top lake.

Ruling Lines: 4 and 5.

Description: Connection. Success! Right pushing rewards. It is good luck to go courting, and take a wife.

The Great Work: In dealing with others, the Superior Individual shows themselves empty of self-referencing (i.e., dividing "self" from "other").

Commentary: The Union of Opposites governs this hexagram. When the weak (broken lines) rises and the strong (solid lines) descends they achieve communion (Knowledge and Conversation). First the ritual of Courting must be properly performed. Men reveal their character by what attracts or repels them. If we observe all manner of sensation, we can commune with Heaven, The World, and all things of Creation (that is, all the elements). The theme of the lines is of sensation in the different parts of the body; although this can also be interpreted as the touches of lovemaking between two partners; the mystical understanding is of gradually approaching a state of divine Communion through meditative trance.

The Lines:

1. Feelings in the toes—worrying about peripheral matters.

2. Feeling in the legs—resist the urge to move—bad luck! Stay still for good luck.

3. Feeling in the loins. He follows the feeling to connect with others foolishly, being manipulated. Shame and regret.

4. * Right pushing brings good luck—but only close friends follow you, because you dither.

5. * Feeling in the spine—no chance to act yet (you lack the vision), but no blame.

6. Feeling in the jaws, don't talk so much!

Notes

Hexagram 32: Heng (pr. "hng")—Persistence

Fire and Air make persistence.

Image: Wind blows and thunder roars.

Ruling line: 2.

Description: Persistence, success, free from mistakes. Right pushing brings rewards. Have a goal!

The Great Work: The Superior Individual stands so firmly that they cannot be uprooted.

Commentary: The balance (of three weak and three strong lines) in this position indicates persistence. It is that which endures unto the end. Heaven and The World move (change) constantly and do not stop; this (and not staying still) is persistence. The inner nature of all under Heaven and The World can be judged by what makes them continue. It is specifically good to have a new goal.

The Lines:

1. Lust of result is bad luck. Seek to be persistent in going deeper (than mere desire) or you will get stuck!

2. * Regret vanishes. You stay true, moving along the middle path.

3. Failing to keep Virtue, disgrace! If you do not restore your persistence you will be rejected everywhere (as one who has broken a vow). No one could stand such inconsistency.

4. No beasts are found in the fields, you are hunting in the wrong place (the strong line is in the wrong position; thus persistence is misdirected).

5. Making a great virtue of marital loyalty: good luck for women, bad luck for men.

6. He retires early, longing for a change in life, but then finds nothing to do. Disaster!

Notes

Hexagram 33: Tun (pr. "dun")—Retreat

Heaven and Earth unite in retreating.

Image: A mountain hidden under the clouds.

Ruling Line: 5.

Governing Lines: 1 and 2.

Description: Retreat. Success! Even being weak, you can persevere in small things, for gain.

The Great Work: The Superior Individual withdraws to a solitary place when things are unfavourable. By keeping distance from lesser people, thus avoiding the need to express wrath, dignity is preserved.

Commentary: Retreat at the right time can lead to success. The weak (broken lines) is rising, but there is still enough strength to achieve something. You can "gain" in the sense of plants growing well if they are properly tended to. The theme of the lines is retreat from battle. Timely action is essential in this hexagram, as the time of retreat is a critical moment.

The Lines:

1. ^ He delays his retreat and is routed. Cornered—disaster! It is useless to seek any goal.

2. ^ Bound in tough ox-hide straps, nothing can untie it! Powerful Will.

3. He is reluctant to give up, for the sake of his subordinates; woe! Danger, exhaustion and illness (are the result). But there is luck for those who care for their servants and concubines.

4. Even though he cares for his subordinates, he must retreat! Good luck for the Superior Individual, bad luck for the Inferior Person (as the Superior Individual was maintaining them).

5. * Orderly retreat. Right pushing, gently, brings good luck. Organize your aims.

6. He retreats with ample time, getting away completely and with ease. Excellent! (you chose the right time).

Notes

Hexagram 34: Ta Kwang (pr. "dah jwung")—Great Power

Fire and Heaven make great power.

Image: Thunder roars over heaven.

Ruling Line: 4.

Description: Great power. Pushing the right brings gain, in spite of any challenges.

The Great Work: The Superior Individual never fails in his rites, nor takes even a single step away from duty.

Commentary: The Superior Individual has great power because of his active nature (the strong lines). Firmness and vigorous movement creates Power. "Great" and "Right" are synonymous here, because only by understanding Truth and being upright can one attain Power.

The Lines:

1. Power in the toes (that is, very peripheral and minor power). If he advances it will be disaster, in spite of all his confidence. It is better to stay calm, humble, and keep silent.

2. Right pushing brings good luck! A strong position.

3. Base men use their power (to abuse others), if Superior Individuals don't use theirs (to protect). Be careful, danger! Use force now, and you may get tricked or stuck, like a ram charging a hedge and getting its horns entangled.

4. * Right pushing rewards, regret vanishes. Entanglement (as in line 3) disappears, and the axle of the cart is firm for going great distances!

5. Making a blood sacrifice for petty reasons—no blame, but ill-advised.

6. Entangled in the hedge, he can go nowhere. But this will ultimately lead to good luck.

Notes

Hexagram 35: Chin (pr. "jin")—Advance

The Sun and The World unite in advancing.

Image: The Sun rises in the east.

Ruling Line: 5.

Description: Advance. The young Prince receives gifts of royal horses and a carriage. He is also given three audiences with the King; well deserved!

The Great Work: The Superior Individual reflects Heaven's Virtue in their very presence.

Commentary: The World is radiant with the Sun's splendour. People in lower positions can advance by attaching themselves loyally to the great and good in higher positions.

The Lines:

1. Advancement seems challenged, with setbacks and demotions. But right pushing brings luck. If you are mistrusted, be patient and generous.

2. Nervous at the time of advancement, sad and worried. Right pushing brings luck. He is given a blessing by the Queen Mother.

3. Trust is won. All in agreement—no regret!

4. Advancing, climbing too fast and quick, he lacks the right skills. Ill-prepared, pushing would have serious risks!

5. * Regret leaves. Be free of lust for gaining, or fear of losing. Seek a goal, all is well.

6. Advancing to the extreme, trying to dominate entire cities. Although there is danger, luck avoids harm. But such behaviour may bring shame, from infamy!

Hexagram 36: Ming Yi (pr. "ming yee")—Dark Injury

The World and Sun unite in dark injury.

Image: The Sun sets in the west and goes under The World at midnight.

Ruling Lines: 2 and 5.

Governing Line: 6.

Description: Darkening; right pushing in spite of hardship brings reward.

The Great Work: The Superior Individual takes care to conceal his light, trying to guide others in secret; yet he still shines!

Commentary: The individual must clothe his inner being with refinement and intellect, while externally appearing humble and obedient. King Wen overcame many great dangers in this way. Win advantage in difficulty by concealing brilliance of mind and character. Despite troubles locked in the heart, unfaltering, fix your Will on righteousness!

The Lines:

1. Darkness while escaping. He panics and flees, going without food for three days. Wherever he goes, his superior hosts will comment, doubting and judging him (for his poor behaviour).

2. * Darkness, an injury in the thigh; but he finds a strong horse and manages to move forward (an ease to troubles). Good luck!

3. Fighting battles in the dark, hunting down the barbarian chief; he is injured but kills his enemy. Gain, but crazy risks should usually be avoided!

4. Doing his duty, he is injured on the left side (betrayed); only then does he see the other's dark heart! He leaves the court and goes off to the wilds (having become disillusioned).

5. * The Prince was injured, but his perseverance led to reward.

6. ^ Endless dark! He turns from shining brilliance to causing darkness. From rising so high, he falls to the farthest depths.

Notes

Hexagram 37: Chia Ren (pr. "jee-ah rn")—Household

Air and Sun make a household.

Image: Air rises from the heat of the Sun.

Ruling Lines: 2 and 5.

Description: The family and home. For women, persistence brings gain.

The Great Work: The Superior Individual speaks with sincere substance, and behaves with constancy on a daily basis.

Commentary: Woman's place is within, man's place is without. Women and men in their proper places accords with Heaven and The World. When parents and children act suitably to their positions, the way of the household runs straight.

(Superficially, this seems to refer to traditional family roles; but mystically it should be understood as an alchemical commentary on the nature of "masculine" and "feminine", "developed" and "developing" qualities in situations and people. Everyone's nature contains both Yin and Yang, the Yin is expressed within, the Yang on the exterior. The accord is the balance of elements, with parallels found in western teachings of the tetragrammaton. The condition of aspiration is masculine, of surrender/attainment feminine.)

The Lines:

1. The household is well-defended against evil. No regrets. Unfailing determination. Take care no one in the family loses his Will.

2. * Nothing works on the outside, but in the home the woman provides for her family. Right pushing brings gain.

3. Family fights; complaints about discipline. Regret and danger, but this may lead to luck. However, women or youths chattering and

fooling around (without working) would only bring shame and disappointment in the end.

4.   Her industriousness makes the family rich—great luck!

5.   * The King's household is his nation. His Virtue is a good influence and ensures the royal family's safety. No cause for worry—good luck!

6.   He is sincere and certain, managing the household with discipline; others are inspired and this brings good luck in the end.

Notes

Hexagram 38: Kuei (pr. "kway")—Separated

```
▬▬▬   ▬▬▬
▬▬▬   ▬▬▬
▬▬▬▬▬▬▬▬▬
▬▬▬   ▬▬▬
▬▬▬▬▬▬▬▬▬
▬▬▬▬▬▬▬▬▬
```

The Sun and Water unite in separating.

Image: The Sun rises and Water falls.

Ruling Lines: 2 and 5.

Description: The separated. You can handle small affairs attentively, and win good luck in those things, at least.

The Great Work: The Superior Individual maintains their difference, while seeking broader unity.

Commentary: Sun moves up, Water moves down. Two women live in the same house and squabble constantly; one is extroverted and pleasure-seeking, the other responsible and introverted. But when they accord, what radiance! The weak (broken line) advances ascending (to line 5); it responds (to the solid lines), thus good luck in small affairs. Though Heaven and The World are separated they are one in activity. Man and Woman are opposites but desire union. Everything has its own separateness (individuality) and has its own purpose to accomplish, but all share the same overarching reality. Timing in applying this hexagram is essential!

The Lines:

1. Regret goes. The lost horse will return on its own, even in evil places. Don't go looking for it. Receive your (evil) opponents, there is no harm.

2. * In the narrow alley, he bumps into his Lord, no blame (for he was on his proper path; and the alley is not a proper place for superiors to find themselves).

3. They destroy his carriage, steal his ox, shave off his hair, and cut off his nose! A bad start; yet later they will become his allies! (Troubles will end, in time.)

4. Separated, he is alone, but then finds a firm friend. Lonely for a long time, she finds a fine caring husband. Trouble but no harm, nor error.

5. * Regret passes! The Barbarian chief eats well at the feast, and seeks peace. The plan is blessed—proceed!

6. On the path, in the rain, he thinks he sees ugly boars and frightening demons. But he should put aside his bow and not delay! If he goes forth he reunites with his wife and has good luck! (Do not waste time fighting illusions, these are the cause of your separation.)

Notes

Hexagram 39: Chien (pr. "jee-en")—Trouble

The Moon and the Earth are trouble.

Image: The Moon rising over a mountain with treacherous terrain.

Ruling Line: 5

Description: Trouble! The South and West (the plains) are good directions; East and North (the mountains) are bad. See the Great Man. Right pushing brings good luck.

The Great Work: The Superior Individual relies on their own cultivation of Virtue, by bringing about revolution within themselves.

Commentary: Trouble, danger ahead. Movement is difficult. To see danger ahead, and avert it, is the nature of wisdom. "South and West" lead to a middle path. "East and North" end in stuckness. The strong (line 5) signifies that persistence brings luck in overcoming troubles and setting the Kingdom aright. There is great opportunity here but right timing is essential!

The Lines:

1. Leaving brings trouble; returning earns praise. Wait.

2. The Minister (King's man) meets trouble after trouble in his service, no blame (because he is trying to serve the King).

3. Going forward would bring trouble, turn back! It is good luck for women when he returns (appreciate inner happiness during troubled times).

4. Going forward would bring trouble, turning back would also bring trouble. Seek to make connections. No blame.

5. * Severe trouble! But then, all his friends arrive to help.

6. Going forward brings trouble, but he overcomes this and returns to great honours (with help from his allies). Seek a great man.

Hexagram 40: Hsieh (pr. "shee-ay")—Shooting

Fire and the Moon unite in shooting.

Image: A dark thunderstorm; later the trees sprout in the aftermath.

Ruling Lines: 2 and 5.

Description: Shooting. Going South and West to relieve besieged peoples is good. If there is no point in either staying put or charging forth, then turn back! If there is a point, even if it is dangerous, go forth with the utmost haste!

The Great Work: The Superior Individual forgives wrongs and pardons criminals, once the shooting is over.

Commentary: Forceful action in the face of danger. Going South and West to relieve people in danger wins many hearts. Return brings luck, and allows the middle path to flourish. Thunder and rain bring forth sprouting plants, renewal. Timely application of this hexagram is essential!

The Lines:

1. The danger has already been relieved. No harm.

2. * A golden arrow (of upright Virtue) kills three foxes with one shot. Right pushing brings gain.

3. Driving a carriage filled with riches, robbers attack him! Pushing (in such an ostentatious way) would be bad luck, and shame! Blame.

4. A bad shot. Dismiss Inferior Persons and trust in sincere friends who arrive.

5. * The Superior Individual shoots true, defeating danger! He may inspire lesser men, though they may flee (in fear, awe or shame) instead.

6. The Prince's shot from the city walls kills a hawk. All is well, you eliminate rebels and end the danger.

Notes

Hexagram 41: Sun—Losing

Earth and Water are losing.

Image: A marshy lake (swamp) at the base of a mountain.

Ruling Line: 5.

Governing Lines: 3 and 6.

Description: Loss, but certainty. Sincerity brings luck, no harm or error. Have a goal. Two plain bowls of food will suffice for a sacrificial rite (i.e., use any small thing). Be moderate.

The Great Work: The Superior Individual keeps his anger in check, and moderates his desires.

Commentary: Loss below, gain above. The way leads upward. "Two small bowls" means use anything that is on hand to start the process of change. The timing matters more (than the technical preparations). There are times when it is good to lose: sometimes the strong (solid lines) must decrease to augment the weak (broken lines), sometimes the weak must decrease to augment the strong. Loss, gain, filling, emptying—each happen in their proper timing.

The Lines:

1. It is not wrong to rush away after work (to help a superior); no harm, if you do not ask too much of yourself.

2. Pushing rightly brings gain, but charging forth rashly brings disaster. Do not give yourself needless losses.

3. ^ Three women together, in search of a man! If one goes off on her own, she will have better luck. Lose bad company.

4. Losing ill-will, she quickly speeds luck along and obtains a fiancée. Happiness, and no error.

5. * A superior enriches you and insists upon it until you cannot refuse. Great luck!

6. ^ Gain, without making others lose. No error. Push rightly for good luck. Have a goal. Gain supporters and not only from one family.

Notes

Hexagram 42: Yi—Gaining

Air and Fire make gaining.

Image: Wind and thunder!

Ruling Lines: 2 and 5.

Governing Lines: 1 and 4.

Description: Gain. Have a goal. Cross the Great River.

The Great Work: The Superior Individual emulates the good, and corrects the bad.

Commentary: Loss above, gain below. If those above are generous, and not arrogant to those below them, their Virtue is illuminated. The route is central and straight, and leads to blessings. When you find a wooden boat (knowledge, the Air element) you may cross the river. Gain is active and smooth, but each gainful activity must happen at its appointed time!

The Lines:

1. ^ Do great works now—gentle good luck, no mistake.

2. * A foreigner enriches you, insisting upon it. Right pushing brings gain. Earlier good works continue and bring reward. The King should offer sacrifice to Heaven, for a blessing.

3. Tragedy is an unfortunate reason for gain, but no blame. Be sincere. When visiting the Prince, bring your seal of office with you!

4. ^ He swears loyalty to the Prince, prudently offering tribute. The Prince will heed his counsel and give him great tasks.

5. * Sincere in his Will, he gives much benefit to all people, who express regard and gratitude for his generosity.

6. He didn't help anyone, so they struck out at him for his hypocrisy and avariciousness. Seeking gain for its own sake—bad luck!

Notes

Hexagram 43: Kuai (pr. "gwy")—Resolve

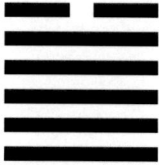

Water and Heaven unite in resolve.

Image: A lake evaporating into the sky.

Ruling Line: 5.

Governing Line: 6.

Description: Resolve. A declaration at the King's court; he is determined to expose the crimes of the Inferior Person. Too much honesty can be dangerous! He needs help against danger from other sincere people. It is unseemly to make a declaration in one's own city while bearing arms. Have a goal.

The Great Work: The Superior Individual can condemn those below, because he is Virtuous, and generous to people. If he does not do so, he invokes condemnation himself.

Commentary: The strong (solid lines) determine the affairs of the weak. He wins admiration in his determination to punish wrongdoing. But it is dangerous (the broken line is above the solid lines). However, the solid lines are gaining in strength (if they join together in a common cause). If he resorts to force (bearing arms) he will lose Virtue (becoming like those he condemns). At the King's court, speaking frankly is a glorious danger! (The theme of this hexagram can be understood externally, or internally as a struggle against one's own Inferior Person).

The Lines:

1. Strong only in the outer. Going forward rashly now will fail and bring harm and shame (those in opposition have too much power and influence). Be sure (before acting)!

2. Being armed, and on alert with staunch allies, he will not have to fear a night attack. Prudent!

3. His face shows his anger—bad luck! The Superior Individual must be firm and go forward with resolve. Even caught in the midst of the storm, muddied and frustrated, in the end he can punish the Inferior Person; and avoid harm and blame to himself, if he's prudent.

4. Being lashed until he limps! A superior offers help, but he feels humiliated and refuses, distrusting motives and ignoring wise advice. Stupid!

5. * Weak but determined, he defeats the Inferior Person; in spite of being doubted by all.

6. ^ Bad luck! In spite of his cries, he cannot escape disaster (because of his own inferior behaviour).

Notes

Hexagram 44: Kou (pr. "go")—Encounters

Heaven and Air make encounters.

Image: Wind blows down from Heaven.

Ruling Lines: 2 and 5.

Governing Line: 1.

Description: Encounters. Women hold power. Do not marry.

The Great Work: The King issues orders that ministers should meet with their subordinates.

Commentary: The weak (broken line) embraces the strong (solid lines). If the feminine (broken line) holds too much power, a marriage right now would not last long. When strength is directed and used wisely (rather than brutishly) all goes well. When a strong teacher meets a receptive student, only then can Enlightenment and Virtue be transmitted. Thus, the right timing in applying this hexagram is vital!

(The symbolism of this hexagram can relate to the relationship between men and women, but also between superiors and subordinates, or teachers and students. The mystical symbolism relates to creating connections/harmony between one's own levels of consciousness.)

The Lines:

1. ^ The carriage has a strong brake. Pushing rightly brings luck, but driving recklessly (in a rush) brings disaster.

2. * Stealing a fish from the kitchen; even to share it with guests, it is shameful. Failing in one's duty.

3. He's been lashed, and limps. But he still walks proudly, avoiding being shamed by others. Trouble, but no great harm.

4. A fish stolen from the kitchen—bad luck! Accusations and conflict. The people are no help as they distrust you and won't speak up on your behalf. Disaster!

5. * Beauty hidden away (within). Heaven blesses you, and an ideal encounter will take place unexpectedly.

6. Alone, butting his head against a wall. Regret, exhaustion. Disappointment at finding no one, but no mistake (there was no one worthy of encountering).

Notes

Hexagram 45: Tsui (pr. "tsway")—Gatherings

Water and The World are gathering.

Image: A lake is fed by rivers from different directions in The World.

Ruling Lines: 4 and 5.

Description: Gathering—success! The King is in the temple, using his Virtue to summon the spirits for the ritual. See the great man. Right pushing brings reward. Make great sacrifices. Have a goal.

The Great Work: The Superior Individual is armed, to prepare against the unforeseen.

Commentary: The solid (strong line) individual in a strong position (line 5) can direct things properly, and guide subordinates. Thus, many will flock to him. The King is in the temple for the good of all. Observe what each thing in creation gathers to itself. The theme of the lines is of a religious (festival) gathering. (The mystical interpretation of the hexagram can be related to the performance of a ritual operation).

The Lines:

1. Sincerity falters: confusion, wrong gathering (with inappropriate people), and dispersion results. Crying, but a friendly hand brings laughter. Advance!

2. Gathering brings luck, and no mistake. With certainty, you can gain by making a sacrifice, however humble.

3. No one to gather with, sighs and despair! No good goal. Advancing would be no mistake, but would bring some regret and disappointment.

4. * Great good luck, and no harm or mistake.

5. * He is respected at the gathering. No mistake (due to his exalted station); but he fails to win their trust. The King will have to work hard to show his Virtue.

6. Sighs and distress, weeping. No harm or mistake, but the gathering fails.

Notes

Hexagram 46: Sheng (pr "shng")—Rising

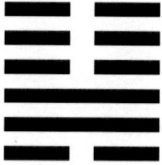

The World and Air unite in rising.

Image: Trees growing from out of the dirt.

Ruling Line: 5.

Governing Line: 1.

Description: Rising—great success! It is essential to see a great man, removing all doubts and worry. Going South brings good luck.

The Great Work: The Superior Individual starts with the small, and builds up much merit doing virtuous things; for the sake of the Great Work.

Commentary: At the right time, the weak (broken line at the bottom) ascends. Our position is far from ideal, but a keen sense of timing can raise us up. Unexpected luck results from seeing the great man. "Going South" implies ascending by fulfilment of what is natural. The theme of the lines is of a step-by-step rise in rank (and spiritual duties).

The Lines:

1. ^ Sure to be promoted—great good luck!

2. As long as you are sincere, it is right to offer even very poor and simple sacrifices at the ceremony of the Summer Solstice (in the South). No harm, happiness results.

3. Promoted to a position in a large city, it is achieved effortlessly.

4. The King sacrifices to the spirits on the holy mountain; you follow and serve his majesty. Good luck, no error. Perform your duty.

5. * Rising up step by step, right pushing brings good luck.

6. Rising in the dark, self-indulgent, he spends great wealth (in bribery) to ascend. Rising by such false methods cannot prevail, he is sure to lose his undeserved power. Seek to discipline yourself with constancy.

Notes

Hexagram 47: Kun (pr. "kwn")Hardship

Water and Moon are hardship.

Image: A dried-up lake-bed.

Ruling Lines: 2 and 5.

Description: Hardship. If you try to push rightly to escape a trapped situation, there will be success. Good luck (only) for the Superior Individual, free from mistakes. Words can be spoken, but they generate no truth.

The Great Work: The Superior Individual, even when trapped, risks their very life to do their Will.

Commentary: Hardship due to being trapped. The real cause may lie hidden. There is no room to move freely. Be joyful even facing danger. The solid line in the middle of both trigrams means that only the Superior Individual can yet persevere (in this situation). As words generate no trust, trying to rely on words to solve things now is useless.

The Lines:

1. Tangled in branches, wandering into a dark vale, lost for three years! Disaster.

2. * Trapped without food or wine (imprisoned, due to prior drunkenness). It is time to make a great sacrifice! Advancing brings great dangers, but no harm. Power, riches and happiness will eventually result (if you atone).

3. Trapped under a rock, stepping on sharp thorns, even when she gets home she finds her suitor is gone. Disaster.

4. Taking a golden carriage, but arriving late (due to hesitation). Shame, but not for long, as someone will soon stand with you.

5. * The harsh Minister abuses the people and is put under house arrest. He will be pardoned, but can only restore trust gradually (by applying moderation). Offer sacrifices!

6. Tangled up in vines and slipping, any action brings regret. But if you truly regret, you can advance, and gain good luck.

Notes

Hexagram 48: Ching (pr. "jing")—The Well

The Moon and Air unite in a well.

Image: A well (Moon trigram) with a wooden bucket (Air trigram).

Ruling Line: 5.

Description: The well. You can move a city, but not a well. The well stays steady and provides water; but if the rope is short or the bucket breaks—bad luck.

The Great Work: The Superior Individual encourages people to work and help each other, giving advice and aid.

Commentary: The city (that which we construct) can be moved, but the well (that which comes from nature) cannot. The Superior Individual's nature should be deep and steady like the well. The theme of the lines is of the trouble when the well (that is, the inner depth) is neglected.

The Lines:

1. Muddy water at the bottom of the neglected well. No animals come to drink the tainted water. Give up.

2. Infested water, and the bucket leaks, double bad luck!

3. The well is cleaned, but no one comes to drink from it, sadly. The King is wise and shares his fortune.

4. The well is being repaired—a delay (no one can drink from it yet), but hopeful progress!

5. * The water is clean and icy cool, there is no need to hide it. Great luck. All is well.

6. The well-rope is found and can be used. A fine achievement. Great luck and great success!

Hexagram 49: Ko (pr. "Ge")—Revolution

Water and The Sun unite in revolution.

Image: The Sun rises over a marshy lake.

Ruling Line: 5.

Description: Revolution. Only when its time has come will it work. Only when finished will the people trust in it. Gentle success. Right pushing brings gain, regret vanishes.

The Great Work: The Superior Individual studies the calendar, understanding change. He guides others through the times and the seasons.

Commentary: Sun and Water are opposed to each other, like two women in the same household, constantly squabbling. One must go. Revolution must come first, then with successful change will public trust gradually be established. When revolution is in accord with Heaven's decree, dynasties can fall and new ones rise. This is a time of epic significance!

(The theme of the lines is of revolution, be it outer or inner.)

The Lines:

1. It is not yet time for revolution. Acting rashly, he is bound in tight ox-hide ropes (arrested, prevented from causing change).

2. The time to begin revolution has come. Advancing brings gain. Good luck, no harm or error.

3. Advancing too quickly brings trouble—disaster! Guard against dangers. Do not go forth (with the revolution) without thinking of others. Be sincere and listen to people. When you hear talk of revolution three times, act!

4. Regret leaves, certainty is gained. He is sincere and thus the change of government succeeds. A new dynasty is established, good luck!

5. * A Great Individual makes change brilliantly! He is like a fierce tiger. He can reveal his Will with certainty, no divination is needed.

6. The Superior Individual helps to make change gracefully. Lesser people will gradually come to his side. If he pushes too radically at this time there are disasters. Being firm but advancing gently brings gain and good luck.

Notes

Hexagram 50: Ting (pr. "ding")—Sacrificial Bowls

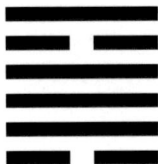

The Sun and Air make sacrificial bowls.

Image: The Sun rises over the treetops. An offering bowl to help duty be performed gently and gracefully.

Ruling Lines: 5 and 6.

Description: A sacrificial bowl—success. Great luck!

The Great Work: The Superior Individual takes the stance that Heaven requires.

Commentary: Wood (the Air Element) and holy fire (symbolic of the Sun) combine to cook the sacrificial offering. Cook well for offerings to the Lord of Heaven, but cook even better to provide for Sages (teachers) and virtuous individuals in The World. The King provides for his Ministers so they will advise him well and care for the Kingdom. (The theme of the lines involves sacrificial/alchemical rites for the production of results, including the creation of a magical child).

The Lines:

1. The bowl is overturned and rotted meat dumped out. If the concubine bears a son, there is no shame in making her a wife! (Get rid of the old and non-functional, use what is practical)

2. The bowl is strong and full of offerings. The former wife is ill and does not object (to the new one). Good luck!

3. The bowl-handles are broken; it is hard to move it! Good food is wasted (you used an unsuitable vessel). But then the rains come regardless (the goal of the ritual succeeds in spite of its failings), washing off regrets and bringing luck in the end.

4. The bowl's legs snap. The Prince's food spills and his robes are stained. A shameful mess—bad luck! (From trying too hard, indicated by the solid line in this position.)

5. * The bowl has golden handles—very suitable (for concrete worldly rituals). Right pushing brings substantial rewards.

6. * The bowl has jade handles—the most suitable (for Heavenly rituals). Great luck! Everything is going your way.

Notes

Hexagram 51: Chen (pr. "Jn")—Thunder

Fire and Fire make thunder.

Image: Continuous roaring thunder!

Ruling Line: 1.

Description: Thunder—success. Great noise, awe and panic, but then there may be laughter and joyful shouting. Some are afraid, but the holder of the sacred cup does not spill the wine. Be prudent, but make a noise that echoes forever!

The Great Work: The Superior Individual, in awe and trembling, seeks to improve themselves.

Commentary: Thunder is frightening but can lead to prosperity (reshaping the world after a storm). It can frighten people for a hundred miles around. That wine is not spilt means that one has been found qualified to lead (the sacrifices). Make a noise (a shock to generate change), considering how others after yourself may continue to use the current of change you have initiated. The theme of the lines is of the state before, during and after a storm (a great period of shock and change).

The Lines:

1. * Thunder, great noise! He is panicked at first, but later feasts. Good luck, happiness and laughter. (Taking advantage of a great shock).

2. Thunderstorm fast approaching. Danger! He drops his goods and heads for the hills. Do not search for the lost riches, they will be regained in seven days.

3. Sudden thunder—panic! Act with haste to avoid harm. Prudent.

4. During the thunderstorm he slips and falls. Muddy road; muddy thoughts.

5. Unpredictable thunder—trouble! He runs around in panic. Careful thought and attention is needed to avoid loss. Maintain discipline in your rites.

6. Thundering chaos! She is panicked, not knowing where to go. Advance brings bad luck. Her neighbour is struck down by the storm; she must be cautious to avoid harm as well. Seeking marriage at this time causes gossip and conflicts.

Notes

Hexagram 52: Ken (pr. "gn")—Stopping

Earth and Earth are stopping.

Image: Two mountains conjoined.

Ruling Line: 6.

Description: Keep the back straight, free the body from its habits. Walking in the courtyard, not seeing any false qualities in others, nor showing any yourself. Meditation—no mistake!

The Great Work: The Superior Individual restrains their base impulses and concentrates on maintaining their present posture.

Commentary: Stop, when it is time to be still. Move, when it is time to move. Remain aware in both movement and stillness. Thus your inner brilliance will shine forth. The theme of the lines relates to the stages in the practice of meditation.

The Lines:

1. Stop the toes—no mistake. Continue cultivating from this beginning.

2. Stopping the legs, though you may feel unhappy at being unable to follow others.

3. Stopping the sex will make your spine too stiff, and give you heartburn. Danger! (You are practising too much restraint.)

4. Stopping the torso, success in avoiding any movement—no mistake! (You are approaching stillness with all of your being.)

5. Stopping the jaw, you avoid speaking nonsense. Order your words carefully to avoid regret.

6. * The highest stillness—base impulses are sincerely redirected and transformed into Virtue. Good luck!

Hexagram 53: Chien (pr. "jee-en")—Gentle Momentum

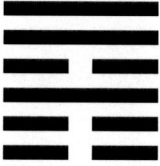

Air and Earth unite in gentle momentum.

Image: A tree (air trigram) on a mountaintop (earth trigram).

Ruling Lines: 2 and 5.

Description: Gentle momentum. A girl marries following all the proper rites. Good luck. Right pushing brings gain.

The Great Work: The Superior Individual cultivates Virtue and thus learns how to improve the practice of rituals.

Commentary: Gradual advance and fortune to those who follow the proper rites, like a virtuous maiden. Going forward this way, success is assured; and even a whole Kingdom can be put in order. The strong solid fifth line indicates that progress has been made and the momentum should continue at this pace.

(The mystical theme of the lines involves the challenges of the aspirant, in pursuit of the True Will; the aspirant here is the maiden, and the True Will her suitor/husband)

The Lines:

1. The maiden moves slowly toward the river. The young son is in trouble (due to inexperience). There is much gossip, but no blame (if one continues forward without rushing).

2. * The maiden moves slowly toward solid ground. There is good food (nourishment), and good luck (material prosperity). Happiness.

3. The maiden moves slowly up the hill. The husband leaves, and does not return. She is pregnant (through adultery)! Shameful. Disaster! Take precautions against intruders (who lead you away from the path of cultivating genuine Virtue).

4. The maiden moves slowly toward the tree, and rests there a while; (its shade is) nurturing and gentle. No harm (in pausing).

5. * The maiden reaches the hilltop, looking (toward the horizon) for her husband. He does not return for three years, but in the end there is good luck and fulfilment. (Pregnancy results, at the proper time).

6. The maiden moves slowly to the city: she is dressed for a great ceremony. Her Will is flawless and chaos cannot prevail.

Notes

Hexagram 54: Kwei Mei (pr. "gway may")—The Eligible Maiden

Fire and Water unite in an eligible maiden.

Image: Lightning striking a lake.

Ruling Line: 5.

Governing Lines: 3 and 6.

Description: The maiden eligible for marrying, fire and water clash. If she advances with inappropriate ways, there is bad luck. No goal is favourable now.

The Great Work: The Superior Individual knows that to achieve an enduring end, they must be aware of their mistakes from the beginning, and stay true to their Love.

Commentary: The eligible maiden: man's end and man's beginning. If there is Love, then the maiden may wed; but if there is no Union (of Heaven and The World), then there will be no prosperity. (As in the case of the previous hexagram, the line meanings here can be understood mystically to reflect challenges on the spiritual path.)

The Lines:

1. The girl is only given as a concubine. The man is lame and cannot walk firmly. But if she aids him, he will aid her—good luck!

2. She is married, but to an evil husband. The blind man tries to see (attempting the impossible). If she meditates, and maintains her duty, she may persevere. (A very difficult situation, but this in no way changes the need to do your duty.)

3. ^ A servant girl is impatient for marriage, but she would do better to accept being taken as a concubine. (Some improvement is better than nothing.)

4. The young maiden grows old waiting for a husband. Her expectations were too high and her actions too few.

5. * The King marries off his youngest daughter. She dresses more humbly than the concubines—Noble! The moon is nearly full (she has great maturity). Good luck!

6. ^ The girl's basket is empty, the man's sacrifice fails. They have no offerings to present for the rites. No goal is favourable, nothing of value. (The prerequisites for proper Union are missing.)

Notes

Hexagram 55: Feng (pr. "fng")—Richness Waning

Fire and the Sun make waning richness.

Image: The Sun at its peak; thunder and lightning striking at once.

Ruling Line: 5.

Description: Richness—success! The Sun-King inspires, but the Sun is at its peak; do not be sad that it (naturally) begins to wane.

The Great Work: The Superior Individual makes judgements and applies strict discipline to himself and others. (He has high expectations of himself and his environment.)

Commentary: First obtaining Virtue, one may then manifest it with rich results. This is the time to let the light of your Virtue shine in The World. The King inspires his people through his respect for them. At its peak, the Sun begins to set. All things follow the same course (in Nature). Humans at their peak being in the process of dying.

The Lines:

1. Meeting a fellow Prince, he stays for ten days, but no more. This earns respect. Proper.

2. Stuck. The Sun has darkened even in mid-day (there is an eclipse). Going now would bring ills and doubts. But with sincerity, trust begins to rise—good luck!

3. He hides in a tent at mid-day, blocking out the Sun, hiding in the dark. He acts as if he broke his right arm (pretending to be useless)—no error. (Hide your abilities at this time.)

4. Stuck. Hiding in a tent at mid-day, blocking out the sun. Meeting an ally of equal Virtue—luck! That will be the time to move.

5. * He shines forth to all, drawing talented allies to himself! He will receive unexpected honours and gifts. Fame won, it is time to celebrate—luck!

6. He builds a great wall around his treasure-house. No one can see him now. He remains reclusive for three years. If he does not show himself soon—disaster! (He has hidden his brilliance for too long.)

(There is a significant similarity in these lines to the description of a "black brother" in the tenth aethyr of Crowley's "The Vision and the Voice".)

Notes

Hexagram 56: Lu—The Traveller

Sun and Earth unite in the traveller.

Image: Sunlight warms a tall peak.

Ruling Line: 5.

Description: The Traveller—gain in small things. Success, if one is modest and cautious. Pushing in travelling brings good luck!

The Great Work: The Superior Individual takes careful attention to administer situations, and prudence in doling out punishment; but he also does not stand for cases to be delayed.

Commentary: The broken line at the fifth place is bordered on both sides by firm solid lines; hence "gain in small things" is possible. Timely application of this hexagram is essential! The theme of the lines is of a traveller on a journey, literal or allegorical.

The Lines:

1. At the start of the journey, he worries about supplies and money, and is miserly. He invites troubles on himself (by expecting the worst and over-reacting).

2. The traveller gets to the inn with his pockets full. He gains a loyal young servant. He should continue to push rightly.

3. The inn burns down, he suffers burns and the servant's loyalty is lost. The traveller was reckless and continuing this way brings trouble. Guard against danger!

4. The traveller stays in one place for a time. He gets new supplies and yet he is still joyless. (Unsatisfied with the current place and situation.)

5. * Hunting, he loses an arrow, but then hits a pheasant (on the second try). He gains praise and titles from superiors. Small loss, great gain.

6. The bird's nest is burnt, the cow is lost in the wild. The traveller laughs at first but later cries. Carelessness leads to loss and there is no one to help or care for you. Woe!

Notes

Hexagram 57: Sun—Surrender

```
▬▬▬▬▬▬▬
▬▬▬▬▬▬▬
▬▬▬  ▬▬▬
▬▬▬▬▬▬▬
▬▬▬▬▬▬▬
▬▬▬  ▬▬▬
```

Air and Air make surrender.

Image: A favourable wind!

Ruling Line: 5.

Governing Lines: 1 and 4.

Description: Willing surrender. Success in small things. Have a goal, visit the Great Man.

The Great Work: The Superior Individual shows leadership and administrates the situation.

Commentary: When people surrender willingly, the King can establish law, and implement his Will. Utmost surrender is required to carry out the Will of Heaven (to take advantage of the natural momentum of the divine wind). The theme is of giving up of efforts (attempts at spiritual surrender).

The Lines:

1. ^ Hesitating in battle, going back and forth, too apprehensive to act decisively. The right pushing of warriors brings advantage. (The Will must be cultivated further, it is not yet time to surrender.)

2. Surrendering excessively (afraid). Consulting with crazy wizards and learning how to work with spirits, he can gain great fortune. No error—despite chaos. (Overcome fear and learn how to boldly deal with inner demons.)

3. Aggravated, he surrenders many times but not with a true Will. Shameful, frustrating, and disappointing. (You cannot fake surrender.)

4. ^ Regret leaves! Hunting, he catches three beasts: one for sacrificial rites, one for tribute to the King, and one for celebration. Great deeds done, solid results by surrendering to the King's Will.

5. * Right pushing, gain. Regret leaves, all is well. A bad start in discipline, but in the end it is implemented well. Acting three days early, good luck for three days after the event.

6. Surrendering excessively, cowering under his bed (afraid). His axe has lost its edge; he loses his travelling money (mental and material conditions for gain are in chaos). Pushing now would bring disaster. Focus on realigning yourself. Guard against trouble.

Notes

Hexagram 58: Tui (pr. "dway")Bliss

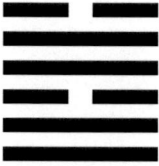

Water and Water are bliss.

Image: Two bodies of water connect and flow one into the other.

Ruling Lines: 2 and 5.

Governing Lines: 3 and 6.

Description: Bliss. Success. Right pushing brings gain.

The Great Work: The Superior Individual joyfully makes friendships, joining in discussion and practice of Art and Virtue.

Commentary: Joyous rapture. When joyously led, people forget their woes. The Superior Individual feels joy at guiding others. Wrestling blissfully with difficulties, one can even forget the woe of death. Bliss' greatest quality is the encouragement it affords (to keep going).

(Mystically, this hexagram relates to the state of Bliss, the "hyperactive" parallel trance state to that of the "hyper-passive" trance state of Surrender.)

The Lines:

1. Untroubled bliss and harmony. He treats others joyously and none doubt him. Good luck and no regrets!

2. * Certainty, bliss. Good luck; he treats others sincerely and regret vanishes!

3. ^ He starts to expect bliss (always). Disaster! (Becoming addicted to bliss and demanding it; getting lost seeking constant "highs" of Bliss instead of seeing it as a vehicle to the Great Work.)

4. Foolishly trying to force future bliss, anxious and troubled. If he can stop pretending to himself and others (trying to convince himself that he can achieve bliss by force), then happiness will

come from unexpected blessings! (Celebrate and appreciate things as they are.)

5. * Trusting in an Inferior Person, and in crumbling situations. He will have problems and danger. (Don't trust promises of easy bliss, don't hold onto situations that no longer work.)

6. ^ Bliss turns into decadence—he seduces others to these false ways, and is ultimately rejected. (When you use bliss to avoid growth rather than encourage it, you settle for cheap glitter without substance.)

Notes

Hexagram 59: Huan (pr."hwn")—Banishing

Air and the Moon unite in banishing.

Image: Wind blowing over the waves of the sea.

Ruling Line: 5.

Governing Lines: 2 and 4.

Description: Banishing—success. The King goes to the temple for sacrifice and uses his Virtue to banish interfering spirits. Cross the great river. Right pushing brings gain.

The Great Work: Ancient Kings built temples to unite the disparate people, offering sacrifices to the Lord of Heaven in places of safety.

Commentary: The strong solid second line has freedom of action (because it is surrounded by broken lines). All is not yet exhausted, but dispersion must first be banished. The King and his Temple are found in the centre. The Air trigram is like a (wooden) boat that allows you to cross dangerous rivers (through mental discipline).

The Lines:

1. With a strong horse one can ride through difficult terrain and help others. Good luck, agreement, cooperation.

2. ^ In chaos, go to the safety of the temple, for firm grounding. Regret will be banished.

3. Banish self-referencing (self-obsessed) thought, unite your Will to the respected King's—no regret.

4. ^ Banishing poor companions, great luck. Calm the mob, unite quarrelling groups into common causes. An Inferior Person cannot achieve this (he cannot even conceive of it!).

5. * Apply discipline so that worry and illness is banished! The King's treasures can thus be shared with the people. No error.

6. In extreme chaos, people gather together, united to banish evil and injury, worry and fear. No error. Banishing is achieved.

Notes

Hexagram 60: Chieh (pr. "jee-eh")—Restraint

The Moon and Water are restrained.

Image: Water restrained by a dam.

Ruling Line: 5.

Description: Restraint—success. But do not restrain too harshly for too long. Right pushing gains.

The Great Work: The Superior Individual makes and uses rites and regulations to maintain Virtue, and encourages those of good report to likewise ascend.

Commentary: Equal number of solid and broken lines create balance. The firm solid lines in the second and fifth places create regulation. If restraint is too extreme, then all restraint will soon be lost (in a dangerous deluge). Take joy in undertaking what is difficult and dangerous. When restraint is properly applied, people and property are protected, and not harmed. The theme is of holding back cautiously in danger.

The Lines:

1. Restrained, he doesn't leave his outer wall; no mistake. When the way is blocked you should remain within.

2. Restrained. He doesn't even leave the inner walls, missing opportunities. Woe! (excessive inward restraint.)

3. He fails to restrain himself! Later, he regrets this, showing good judgement. The harm ceases—no mistake.

4. Restraint and peace—success! Prudent.

5. * Voluntary restraint at first—good luck. Then (later) it is time to move and win respect and praise.

6. Harsh restraint! Pushing in this brings disaster. End the way of excessive restraint, and regret will leave.

Notes

Hexagram 61: Gong Fa (pr. "Joong Fuh")—Divine Law

Air and Water unite in divine law.

Image: Wind blowing over a lake.

Ruling Line: 5.

Governing Lines: 3 and 4.

Description: Sincerity, certainty. Even piglets and river fish (lucky symbols; in some versions the latter are translated as "dolphins") will be moved by it. Cross the great river effortlessly. Right pushing brings gain.

The Great Work: The Superior Individual puts careful attention into judgement, and holds back from issuing death sentences (i.e., judging too harshly).

Commentary: The broken lines are in the safe middle of the hexagram. The strong solid lines are at the visible exterior, and also in the central positions (lines 2 and 5). With Divine Law you can win the confidence of all creatures (hence even piglets and river fish will be moved by it). Crossing the great river is effortless because you have mastered the wooden boat (the Air trigram, the mind).

The Lines:

1. Maintain your heavenly nobility—good luck. To seek out anything else will only bring worry. Stand alone.

2. Birds sing to each other; soon the sound of chicks will follow. Someone will wish to share good wine with you. Follow Nature's Law, with Will situated in your heart. Share sincerity.

3. ^ Insecure, he faces a strong enemy! He dithers about what to do, making much noise, attacking, fleeing, crying, or singing. (Dispersion, being disconnected from Divine Law.)

4. ^ Horses stray, just before the full moon, going free their own way (apart from their mates). No harm or error in this (it is their natural Will).

5. * Certainty generates momentum. Sincerity generates good communication with others. No mistake.

6. The bird calls too loud and flies too high. Bragging to the Heavens—hubris! Continuing brings bad luck. Guard against trouble.

Notes

Hexagram 62: Hsiao Kuo (pr. "shee-au gwo")—Small Gains

Fire and Earth unite in small gains.

Image: Thunder rumbles on a mountaintop.

Ruling Lines: 2 and 5.

Description: Small gains—success. Right pushing brings gain. Small goals are possible to achieve now, large goals are not. High-flying birds sing out of tune, they should find somewhere to land. The humble, and not the strong, have good luck now.

The Great Work: The Superior Individual makes a point to be more reverent, feel more sorrow and grief, and be more thrifty in his expenses (that is, he imitates the ways of the Inferior Person).

Commentary: There are times when it is appropriate to behave in a small manner. The broken lines in the second and fifth places signify that it is possible to achieve small goals. The strong solid lines at the third and fourth places would overstretch themselves in this situation and fail. A high-flying bird can't sing harmoniously. Those trying to ascend at this time will meet with hardship; those descending find their way smooth.

The Lines:

1. The high-flying bird augurs bad luck. Disaster, nothing can be done to avoid it.

2. * In the cemetery, to honour ancient ancestors, he sees his mother's ghost! Trying to reach the King, he is instead only met with the Minister (he is not ready to progress further until first dealing with intermediate issues).

3. Unless he takes care, one of his subordinates will kill him—disaster! Do not avoid simple attention and precautions. (Some small care will avoid very big problems.)

4. Harassing her, being too forward, there will be trouble. Do not show off. Hide your talents but hold on to your determination.

5. * High dark clouds from the west, too high, no rain. The Prince shoots the vicious beast in the cave! (In spite of appearances, this is the right time to act.)

6. Smugly, he gets too far ahead and fails to meet his ally. A bird who flies apart from the flock is sure to be shot. Disaster, injury!

Notes

Hexagram 63: Chi Chi (pr. "jee jee")—After Ending

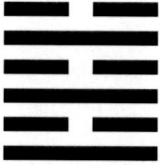

The Moon and the Sun unite after ending.

Image: The Moon rises as the Sun sets. The evening at dinner time, the end of the day.

Ruling Line: 2.

Description: After ending. Success even in the smallest details. Right pushing brings gain. If one is not prudent, the good luck at first will turn to chaos at the end.

The Great Work: The Superior Individual considers future troubles with careful thought, and takes advance precautions.

Commentary: Things are as good as they can be: there is an equal balance of strong and weak lines, and they are all in their proper position (all solid lines in odd places, all broken lines at even places). Good luck at this time, but if we do not determine to seek out and embrace new change, entropy will overtake us. Whenever something reaches its peak, it must inevitably decline. Momentum will wane, and things will collapse into disorder. Thus, do not cling too long to the present situation. Take prudent care against collapse, and seek out change (in spite of your present comfort).

The Lines:

1. He applies the brakes to the chariot's wheels to slow down its descent. Prudent.

2. * The Lady loses her chariot-drapes, and cannot go out. She shouldn't seek them out; they will be restored to her in seven days (be proper, don't draw attention to yourself, let things fix themselves).

3.   The Great King invaded barbarian lands and conquered them in three years of heavy battle. Tiring, but Inferior People would have failed at such a task. Do important things yourself. Persevere to the very end, in spite of exhaustion.

4.   Rags hidden under fine silk (a trick to mask worthless goods). Be cautious, and suspicious of appearances. Guard against trouble.

5.   The Eastern nation sacrifices a bull, but gains less than the more sincere Western nation, even though the latter's sacrifice was less ostentatious. (This line is clearly a reference to the decadent and hypocritical Shang Dynasty, which was in the East; as opposed to the poor and modest but sincere and virtuous Zhou, who eventually overthrew them. Note that in his lifetime, King Wen (who is said to have written these lines) was chief of the Zhou, and a prisoner of the Shang King).

6.   He crosses the river and the water reaches his head. Danger! Being unprepared, chaos rises.

Notes

Hexagram 64: Wei Chi (pr. "way jee")—Before Ending

The Sun and the Moon unite before ending.

Image: The Sun rises as the Moon declines; it is not yet noon.

Ruling Lines: 5.

Description: Before ending—success, if you work hard for it. The little fox tries to cross the frozen river, but gets its tail wet before it can finish crossing the ice. No goal is favourable now (if you seek only the easy way).

The Great Work: The Superior Individual takes care to distinguish between things, before ordering them each into their proper place.

Commentary: The fox crossing the frozen river must be cautious (this is an old Chinese proverb). If he tries to rush to the end he will fall into the water. The image suggests we are not yet at the middle of the situation. Our affairs cannot be rushed to completion. The lines are all in the wrong position (the solid lines are all in even places, the broken lines are all in odd positions); but (because there are an equal number of solid and broken lines) they can complement each other in order to succeed (with hard work). The theme of the line descriptions is one of trying to cross a frozen river.

The Lines:

1. The fox gets its tail wet, embarrassing! Failing to be prudent and wisely judge chances, distance, or timing.

2. Putting the brakes on the chariot to slow it down (on icy terrain).

3. The ford is not yet finished. If he rushes ahead—danger! Crossing the river (at the proper pace) brings gain, in spite of risks.

4. Right pushing brings gain, regret vanishes. He leads his army like a thunderbolt to attack barbarian lands! It takes great work, but

three years later he conquers, and is rewarded with titles and vast lands.

5. * Right pushing brings luck, and regret vanishes. The Superior Individual shines bright and true, winning people's hearts. Good luck!

6. Trusting others, and having their trust, you can feast—no harm. But if you indulge until your head is wet (with drunkenness) you will lose that trust, and gain shame. (Refine your rapture, exceed by delicacy, be subtle in your joy.)

Notes

Chapter Four

Advanced I Ching Studies

Permutations of the Hexagrams

At this point, we have already explored the basics of the I Ching: the text itself, and the fundamentals of how to cast and interpret a standard I Ching reading. For someone using the I Ching casually as a tool for divination, this is essentially all that is needed. However, this is only the tiny tip of a very large iceberg of the incredible wealth of knowledge, contemplation, and imagery found in the mysteries of I Ching. These mysteries can be studied carefully to obtain a much more profound knowledge of the way the I Ching hexagrams relate to each other; and as the hexagrams represent different situations in Time/Space, this type of study allows us to understand the particular ways phenomena in existence are interconnected.

The first, oldest, and most important set of advanced studies in the I Ching is found in what are called the "permutations". These are the ways that a hexagram can be transformed into another hexagram. One of these permutations has already been explained: the "resulting hexagrams" that are formed when changing lines in a casting are shifted into their opposite. Every changing line becomes its opposite, and in this way a new hexagram (generally understood to be the "future" hexagram of that particular casting) is created. This permutation is of obvious significance in divination, because it represents the way a particular hexagram casting is in the process of transforming in that specific instant into another kind of hexagram.

The other hexagram permutations are not specific to an individual casting, but rather are static permutations: the way a specific hexagram will always be connected to certain other hexagrams through specific transformations. Studying these will not always be of direct use to a specific divination, but will provide powerful insights for contemplation which reveal certain details about a given hexagram and its qualities; by virtue of comprehending what hexagram it emerges from, which is its complementary pair, which represents the same forces in opposite positions, and which in reversed positions.

Overturned Hexagrams and Opposite Hexagrams

The first sets of permutations that should be observed in advanced I Ching studies are what are called the "overturned" hexagrams and the "opposite" hexagrams. These are particularly important because they directly relate to the way the I Ching is ordered in its standard text. This ordering or "sequence" is called the "King Wen Sequence", because allegedly King Wen was the one who arranged them in this way. Historically, we know this is almost certainly not true, and that in fact this sequence predates the time of King Wen. It is the oldest and most common sequence of the I Ching.

It should be noted that there are other sequences: some ancient versions of the I Ching do not appear to have the hexagrams in any special mathematical or symbolic order, but possibly in an order that made the hexagrams easy to memorize based on their names. Later on, the great I Ching master Shao Yung ordered the hexagrams according to binary code. However, the King Wen sequence is the most important, and has become the established canonical sequence of ordering the hexagrams.

Ironically, many inexperienced students of I Ching can use the I Ching for years without realizing the significance of this particular arrangement of the Hexagrams. The King Wen sequence is not as obvious as the binary sequence, and thus it leads the I Ching student to think it may just be random. In fact, the King Wen sequence contains within it a series of profound symbolic interconnections.

The first and most apparent rationale for the King Wen sequence becomes immediately apparent when you start to observe the ordering as a set of thirty-two pairs. Look at hexagrams #1 and #2, #3 and #4, #5 and #6, etc., all the way to #63 and #64. Compare each hexagram in a pair to the other. What you will find is that every single pair is either an "overturned" hexagram pair or an "opposite" hexagram pair.

An opposite hexagram is generated when you take all the lines in a hexagram and change them into their opposite. So for example, if you look at hexagram #27, "Eating" (Fire below, Earth above):

and change it into its opposite, you get hexagram #28 "Excess (weight)" (Air below and Water above):

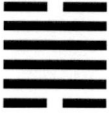

This tells you that there is a connection between these two hexagrams, that they are oppositional to each other; and there is much that you can contemplate in these paired symbols. To begin with, even the very titles are significant: Eating implies hunger, lack. Excess (weight) implies obesity, saturation. The imagery of the two hexagrams are very telling: "Eating" shows solid lines on the outer edges with a wide gap of broken lines in between them. The imagery evoked is literally that of an open mouth, waiting to receive food. "Excess (weight)" shows weak broken lines on the outer extremes while the middle is over-full of solid lines. The traditional imagery of this hexagram is of a beam that is under a weight that is just too heavy to hold it; but you can also almost visualize in the hexagram imagery a portly man, his stubby legs at the bottom just too weak to handle his bumbling bulk. The opposition of the trigrams are also notable: in #27 you have potent Fire below and solid Earth above. In western elemental symbolism these are the higher masculine (the Y of YHVH) below, and the lower feminine (the final H of YHVH) above; in the traditional Chinese "family" of the trigrams, Fire is known as the "eldest son" while Earth is known as the "youngest son". In #28 the Fire is burned up into Air (the Y becoming a V; or the "eldest son" becoming the "eldest daughter"), while Earth is washed away into Water (the lesser feminine H-final becoming the greater feminine first-H of YHVH; or the "youngest son" becoming the "youngest daughter").

On the other hand, an overturned hexagram is generated when you take a hexagram and put it upside down; so that line 6 of the first hexagram becomes line 1 of the new hexagram, line 5 becomes line 2, line 4 becomes line 3, etc. For example, if you look at hexagram #23 "Shedding" (The World below, Earth above):

and overturn the hexagram, you generate hexagram #24 "Return" (Fire below, The World Above):

The overturned hexagram pairs are not directly oppositional, but represent instead the inverse forces of one another. Once again, here we can contemplate significance in the names, the trigrams, and the lines. The core concept of hexagram #23 is of "Shedding", of a situation of corruption where things must be shed off in order to initiate reform. Hexagram #24 marks "Return", where we can understand that the period of crisis has ended and now strength is just starting to return. In the constitution of the trigrams we see that both trigrams have The World; but in "Shedding", The World is below and Earth is above. Both of these are passive forces, and the greater of the two is at the base of the situation. In "Return", the weight of Earth is gone, and now The World and its passivity is no longer the foundation; it has the appearance (in comparison) of moving away from the base of things. The situation is still not ideal, but now a Fire has been lit under the hexagram and energy and motion is starting to build up!

In the line imagery, you can see that both hexagrams have only a single solid Yang line, but in Shedding that line is at the very top, at the "end" of the hexagram; you almost get the sensation that it risks slipping away. The sixth position is at the very end, at the periphery of the line structure. So in this hexagram, force is being lost in a time of great weakness. In Return, you find the single solid line at the very bottom, at the base. The first line in a hexagram represents a force that is also outside; it is only at the very beginning, it has not yet achieved a central part of the process. But the sensation evoked by the solid line in this position is that the strong line is on the way up; it is going to start moving into a more central position, possibly bringing more strong lines behind it. Thus in hexagram #23, the weak has almost completely overwhelmed the strong; while in #24, the strong has returned and will now begin to restore strength to a weakened environment.

To understand the King Wen sequence, you must consider opposite and overturned hexagram pairs. Every single pair in the King

Wen sequence is either an overturned pair or an opposite pair; the overturned pairs are the majority, while the opposite pairs are formed by those hexagrams which would otherwise be identical to each other if overturned. In this way, all phenomena in time and space are understood as either a two-part process of coming and going (or going and coming); or as two directly oppositional forces in interaction with one another. By studying the King Wen sequence in its constituent pairs, you can greatly deepen your understanding of the hexagrams involved and the processes they represent.

Of course, it can also be worthwhile to observe the opposite hexagram pair of each hexagram that isn't already paired to its opposite in the King Wen sequence.

Nuclear Hexagrams

The next most significant set of permutations are the so-called "nuclear hexagrams". They are called this because they are the hexagrams within other hexagrams (found in the "nucleus" of a hexagram). The way to create a nuclear hexagram from another hexagram is as follows: take the second, third and fourth line of a hexagram, and make this the lower trigram of your new hexagram. Then take the third, fourth and fifth line of the hexagram, and make this the upper trigram of your new hexagram.

So a standard hexagram will have six lines; from the bottom counting up, we'll call them lines 1-6:

6

5

4

3

2

1

We now generate the lower trigram of the nuclear hexagram by copying lines 2, 3, and 4 of the regular hexagram; then we generate the upper trigram by copying lines 4, 5, and 6 of the regular hexagram. So the nuclear will look like this:

5

4

3

4

3

2

For example, if we were to look at the hexagram #30, "Flaming Majesty":

This hexagram is Sun below and Sun above. If we first look at lines 2, 3, and 4, we get the Air trigram. Lines 3, 4, and 5 make the Water trigram. Thus we discover that the nuclear hexagram of #30 is #28 "Excess" (weight):

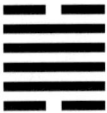

These are "nuclear" hexagrams because they consist of a folded-up or interlaced (a mathematician might call it a "hyper-dimensional") hexagram that is contained entirely within the first hexagram; it does not use lines 1 or 6, so it does not exist in the outer fringes of the hexagram, only within the core of the hexagram.

There is a great deal of misunderstanding regarding the nuclear hexagrams: often, many I Ching students I've encountered (of the minority who know about nuclear hexagrams) seem to think that any hexagram might be a nuclear hexagram, when in fact this is not the case. This misconception is largely due to the fact that even many of those books or translations of the I Ching that mention nuclear hexagrams do not really seem to understand the concept or the underlying mathematics. Consequently, some students treat a nuclear hexagram as an extra part of a casting, using it the way one might draw another Tarot card in a Tarot reading, to describe "hidden influences". While this is not altogether wrong, the nuclear hexagrams do not describe some kind of hidden influences particular to the situation of a casting (much less of the person getting the casting), but rather they represent a fundamental root of the hexagram itself.

The key to understanding nuclear hexagrams is this idea of hyper-dimensionality: imagine that the sixty four hexagrams do not all exist at the same level of space-time; if you projected the sixty four hexagrams as a multidimensional object, you would end up with an image that looks similar to a lattice with several levels, or a sphere that folds in on itself in more than three dimensions. The patterns of the nuclear hexagrams are key to comprehending this, and the King Wen sequence (the regular ordering of the hexagrams in the canonical I Ching) takes this into account.

To understand this, let's look at the pattern of nuclear hexagrams in reverse. There are only four hexagrams from which ultimately all other hexagrams derive (that is, all other hexagrams have one of these four as their nuclear hexagram, or as their nuclear hexagram's nuclear hexagram). These are Hexagrams #1, #2, #63 and #64. You'll note that #1 is all solid lines, #2 is all broken lines, and #63 and #64 are alternating solid and broken lines. You'll also note that these are hexagram pairs, and that the King Wen sequence thus begins and ends with the two pairs.

It is also worthwhile to note that of these four fundamental nuclear hexagrams, #1 and #2 are opposite to each other and #63 and #64 are opposite to each other. Yet at the same time, #1 and #2 are self-contained qualities. They represent a basic force that remains fundamentally itself; thus the nuclear of #1 is #1, and the nuclear of #2 is #2. It is not that they do not change, because everything is change; but that unless modified by change (as can happen in reality, and can be measured in an I Ching divination casting) to mutate into a different hexagram, in an idealized state free of any other influence they would constantly change into themselves: #1 is the fundamental point, #2 the fundamental space. On the other hand, #63 and #64 represent a cycle of eternal recurrence; the nuclear of #63 is #64, and the nuclear of #64 is #63. Free of any outside influences, they would constantly change into each other. Sun and Moon, Moon and Sun;

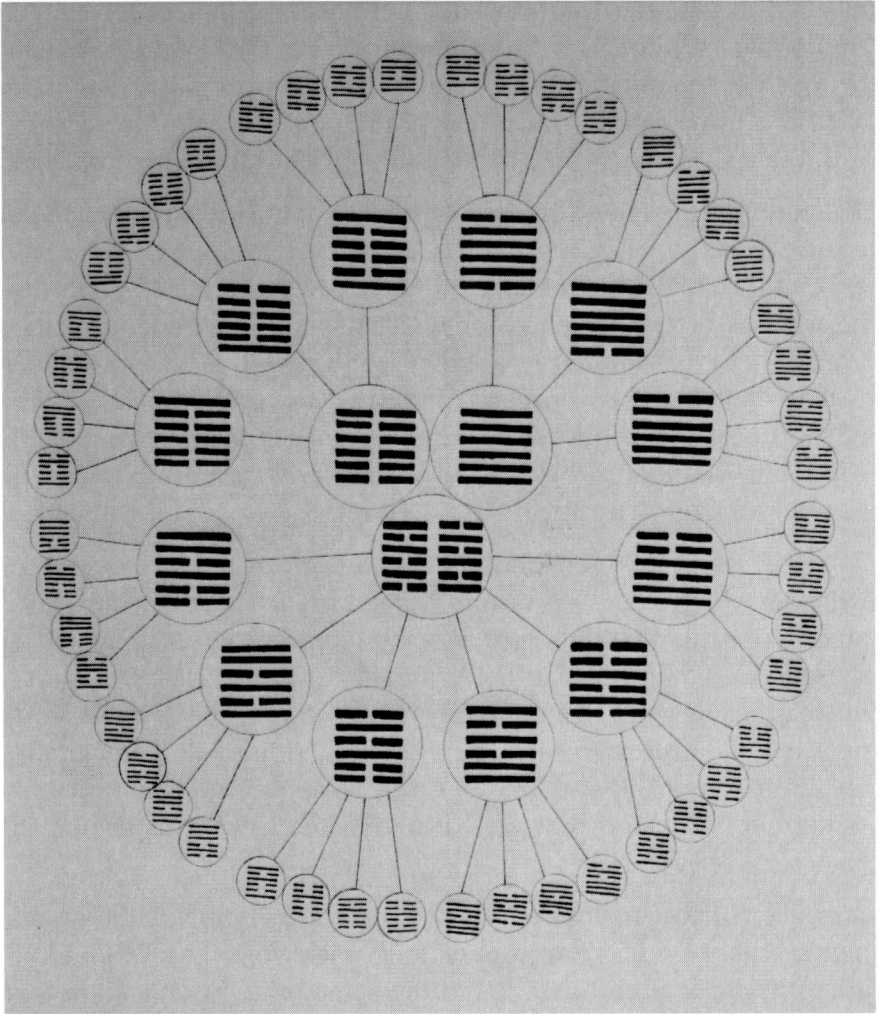

Above: the pattern of the nuclear hexagrams, projected as a circle. To visualize this in a more authentic fashion, the circle would actually need to be a multidimensional sphere.

Yin without turning into Yang without, Yang within turning into Yang without. They represent the flow of time at its essence: the old and the new, ending and beginning. Thus in these four hexagrams (the first and last two pairs of the King Wen sequence), you have the fundamental "nuclear forces" that define all of space and time.

The following reference chart allows you to quickly look up the nuclear hexagram of any hexagram:

Hexagram #	Is a Nuclear Hexagram of:
1	28, 43, 44
2	23, 24 27
63	38, 40, 54
64	37, 39, 53

The following hexagrams are all nuclear hexagrams of #1, 2, 63 or 64, and are in turn nuclear hexagrams of:

Hexagram # (nuclear)		Is a Nuclear Hexagram of:
23	(2)	3, 8, 20, 42
24	(2)	4, 7, 19, 41
27	(2)	29, 59, 60, 61
28	(1)	30, 55, 56, 62
37	(64)	6, 10, 47, 58
38	(63)	5, 9, 48, 57
39	(64)	16, 21, 35, 51
40	(63)	15, 22, 36, 52
43	(1)	14, 32, 34, 50
44	(1)	13, 31, 33, 49
53	(64)	12, 17, 25, 45
54	(63)	11, 18, 26, 46

Reversed Hexagrams

There is one other form of permutation that can be worthwhile to examine, and this is what is called a "reversed hexagram". Not to be confused with overturned or opposite hexagrams, a reversed hexagram works by taking the constituent trigrams of a hexagram and reversing their positions. For example, starting from hexagram #62, "Small Gains", which is Earth below and Fire above:

▤

Its reversal would be formed by putting Fire below and Earth above; thus the reverse is #27, Eating:

▤

As with the oppositional or overturned hexagrams, the reversed hexagram permutation can reveal certain mysteries about both hexagrams involved. The elements of both hexagram will be the same ones, but the change in their position affects their relationship and the structural appearance of the lines. "Small Gains" feels a bit claustrophobic; the strong lines are right in the middle of the hexagrams, the central (second and fifth) lines and the outer (first and sixth) lines are all broken lines. The hexagram feels like it is introverted, looking in, and this matches its advice about the need of the Superior Individual to hide one's greatness.

On the other hand "Eating" is wide open in the middle, its "mouth" formed by the two strong lines at either outer edge; it implies something very extroverted, an open mouth seeking to be fed. Here Fire is below, engaged in intercourse with Earth, warming it and making it more volatile than usual; while in "Small Gains" the trigrams seem to be back-to-back to each other, facing in opposite directions, Fire does not intermingle with Earth enough to create any great explosions (so only small gains are possible).

Directional Theories of the I Ching

In the course of its history, the I Ching has been used quite heavily for predictive fortune telling of different varieties. As this was underway, various models were gradually developed for understanding the relationship between trigrams and hexagrams, and specific details that could be used to aid in prediction. Different systems tried to map specific trigrams or hexagrams to seasons, dates and times, to parts of the body, or to compass directions.

The latter is particularly significant because it overlaps with another Chinese art that has recently become popularized (in certain forms) in the West: Feng Shui. Originally intended as a system for the auspicious construction of buildings or other structures (a kind of fortune-telling for architecture), in the West the specific brand of Feng Shui that has become popular is largely concerned with interior designing (possibly because it is easier to rearrange your furniture in order to avoid bad luck, than to remodel your entire house).

The development of Feng Shui played a significant role in codifying the importance of directions for assessing the eight trigrams; and this has led to two very different arrangements of the trigrams along compass points. The first of these is the "Earlier Heaven" arrangement, which was attributed to Fu Xi but in fact (ironically) is almost certainly the later invention of the two; possibly created by Shao Yung or one of his pupils (as with most of Shao Yung's theories on the I Ching, it is notable for trying to follow a logical mathematical sequence):

In this image, as is standard in ancient China, the upper compass point is actually south, and thus the Heaven trigram is pointing south and The World trigram points north. These also correspond in seasons to Summer and Winter, respectively. The Sun trigram thus points east, and the Moon west; and both represent Spring and Autumn respectively.

There is a mathematical code inherent in the choice of trigrams: if you count every solid line in a trigram as "1" and every broken line as "2", then adding the total number values of any two trigrams at opposite compass-points will give you a total of 9. This is thus an equivalent talisman to the "magical number squares" which were popular in the East and West alike.

The other arrangement is called "later heaven" and is attributed to King Wen:

As before, south is at the top of this arrangement. Here it is the Sun trigram that faces south, while Moon is north; Fire is east while Water is west. The seasons correspond to the same directions as before: south is Summer, north is Winter, east is Spring, and west is Autumn. This attribution has none of the mathematical elegance of the former; the explanation given is that the "earlier heaven" arrangement expresses the "ideal universe" of perfect order, while the "later heaven" arrangement expresses the world as it actually is. Thus, in Feng Shui the "earlier heaven" arrangement is usually only used for burial grounds, tombs and religious monuments; while the "later heaven" arrangement is used for the building of houses (and, in a more simplistic way, for modern "interior designer"-style Feng Shui).

These correspondences to directions and seasons are included here mainly because they may be of some use for predictive divination; if a question asked requires an answer in the form of a direction or even a particular time period, examining the direction or season to which the trigram corresponds (particularly to the trigram that is most central in the divination, for example the one with the most significant changing line) could provide a predictive answer (ostensibly using "earlier heaven" for esoteric matters, and "later heaven" for more practical matters). When one considers that if the trigrams of either arrangement are spread out over the course of the year each line would then correspond roughly to a fifteen-day period, one could also use this to make very specific predictions. For example, if the bottom line of the Heaven trigram in the "earlier heaven" arrangement is taken to mean the first fifteen days following the Summer solstice, this would mean that a key changing second line of the Air trigram in a divination casting would correspond to the first-half of the third month of Summer.

Correspondences

From at least the time of Aleister Crowley, there has been a concerted effort among western practitioners of occultism to try to map the I Ching system to western symbolic languages; to find what are called "correspondences", understanding which symbol in the I Ching system corresponds to equivalent symbols in the western occult system. In fact, it could be argued that there were some minor attempts to do this even earlier, as early as when the first Jesuits discovered the existence of the I Ching; at that time, they were seeking evidence of the Christian God's inspiration in foreign (non-Christian) culture, and Jesuits in China felt that the mathematical and symbolic genius of the I Ching might have been one such piece of evidence. They attempted to find connections between the symbolism and philosophy of the I Ching and the metaphysical system of Catholic dogma.

For practitioners of western magick, correspondences are an essential concept, as they allow the western magician to tie-together all phenomena into a single common language; however, the question persists of how much of what we consider "correspondences" are absolute truths and how much are relative cultural values. Is the Qabalistic system of the Tree of Life a "real" concept outside of human conception, or even outside of western cultural paradigms? And if it is not, then can there be some kind of value in even attempting to use correspondences at all, much less to try to incorporate correspondences from other cultural backgrounds that are not western?

It is fairly clear to anyone capable of understanding the concept of symbol that there is no great invisible tree out in space any more than there is a giant Yin-and-Yang "Taiji" symbol out rotating somewhere in space. Just as the periodic table is not something that literally exists somewhere, but rather is a way of organizing the elements of chemistry; just like the letters d-o-g do not make up a literal dog, but a way of symbolically representing the concept of "dog"; likewise metaphysical systems (be they the Qabalistic Tree of Life, the trigrams and hexagrams of the I Ching, the Norse Tree of Yggdrasil, or the six-worlds model of Tantric Buddhism, etc.) are not literal representations of reality but systems by which we can organize concepts in the universe. To conceive of these as literal is to mistake a filing system for the things it is organizing.

If this is the case, it means that neither western nor eastern systems of metaphysics are inherently "right" or "wrong", they can only be judged by their utility. Certainly, the complex metaphysical system of the I Ching has utility, as does the system found in the hermetic/ qabalistic Tree of Life. If all things were equal, it would be difficult to reach any conclusion about whether one system has more "utility" than another; fortunately no such objective conclusion is necessary. What is important instead is the fact that if one is a westerner, there is an added value to the western system, in that the western occult tradition is something westerners are immersed in. Obviously, if one is already a practising occultist, one will have a first-hand experience with this symbolic language; and thus there will be value in trying to understand correspondences between the I Ching and the Western Occult Tradition, rather than having to "reinvent the wheel" by undertaking a full immersion into the Taoist/Confucian cosmology. Even if one is not an experienced western magician, however, there is a value in trying to put the I Ching into a context of western symbolism. This is because even someone who has never studied any kind of western esoteric teachings whatsoever will still have a natural familiarity with its symbols. Those symbols are all around us in the West: they're found in the major western religions, in our mythology, legends, literature, and art. Much like someone could use common phrases in English culture like "I haven't slept a wink" or "give the devil his due" without realizing it comes from Shakespeare, and "you're the apple of my eye" or "he's the salt of the earth" without realizing that these come from the King James Bible, one will likewise have subconscious cues when it comes to western symbolism. Westerners will have an inherent and unconscious connection through immersion to the ideas of what western symbols of the Elements, planets, mythological deities, even magical words or images represent, without having a full and informed intellectual knowledge of western occultism. It is one of the reasons why the Tarot cards (a treasure-house of western esoteric imagery, which might not even have originally been intended as such!) make such an impact and evoke sensations even in people who have had no formal training in Tarot study.

There is no essential requirement that we map correspondences between the I Ching system and western occultism; the I Ching stands perfectly fine in its own right and can be used by westerners without ever bothering with such mapping. However, the exercise of trying to make these links can certainly help to deepen our contemplations on the I Ching from a westerner's perspective.

I will also note that none of these correspondences should be understood as definitive; that is not to say that there cannot be definitive correspondences, but that at this point these are only the working models and theories that I have found some value in exploring over the last two decades. There is still a great deal of work that can be done before any conclusions can be reached on most of these subjects.

I Ching Trigrams and Magical Elements

The first, simplest, and most direct level of correspondence between the I Ching and western symbolism is found in the trigrams. In fact, in this book I have already been making use of "correspondence" in the way I have titled the trigrams. The standard translation of the eight trigrams found in most versions of the I Ching are Heaven, Earth, Fire, Water, Thunder, Lake, Wind, and Mountain. In this edition, I have titled each of these as follows: Heaven, The World, Sun, Moon, Fire, Water, Air and Earth. It is important to note that this is not a foreign mislabelling of the original trigrams, because each trigram has its own set of various symbols associated with it, and each of the titles I have used are in fact traditional Chinese attributions for those trigrams; it happens that they also function very effectively to explain how each trigram relates to the western elemental system.

At first glance, it would seem tricky to incorporate a system of eight elements into the western system of four classical elements. However, this becomes simpler if you comprehend that there are two groups of trigrams: there are the "terrestrial trigrams" which are the four classical elements (Fire, Water, Air, and Earth), and then there are the "celestial trigrams" which are the four elements reflected in the higher sphere (Heaven, The World, Sun, and Moon).

It should be noted that the nature of this division is not purely arbitrary or even aesthetic. It is also directly in the geometry of the trigrams themselves. Look at the celestial trigrams: Heaven and The World are both perfectly harmonious systems within themselves, pure Yang or pure Yin. The Sun and the Moon are one stage lower, they have a single line that is different in them, but this line is in the middle, balanced there between the two outer lines. On the other hand, if you examine the terrestrial trigrams, you will observe that they are all inherently unbalanced by themselves; they too have one line that is not like the others, but now that line is always at an extreme, either on top or at the bottom. The King Wen sequence itself makes note of this, as the first two and last two hexagrams of the sequence consist of only celestial trigrams; these four hexagrams are also the four "core" nuclear hexagrams, the ones from which all other hexagrams are derived.

One way to understand the western correspondences of these two groups of trigrams is through the model of the pentagram, the five-pointed star which in western occultism is connected to the elements. The four lower points of the pentagram are tied to the four classical elements; the top point of the pentagram is "Spirit", the "quintessence" (literally "fifth element"), which is consciousness beyond matter (and yet, through the pentagram, tied to matter).

With the eight trigrams of the I Ching, we can think of the four "terrestrial" trigrams as representing the four basic elements, and the four "celestial" trigrams are likewise the four elements but seen through the perspective of spirit; they are the four basic elements infused with the "quintessence".

Thus we can think of the Moon as Earth elevated by spirit; the Sun as Air sparked by the energy of spirit; The World as Water in the full depth of spirit, and Heaven as Fire refined into the creative power of spirit. One cannot just think of the "celestial trigrams" as a merely "stronger" version of a terrestrial element, however. The difference is that the terrestrial elements are self-contained; each is only their own element, albeit with reflections in material nature.

The Earth trigram is only earth, not fire, water, or air. But it manifests in matter in a number of ways: mountains, hills, rocks, solidity in all its forms; as well as stillness and stubbornness in human beings.

The Air trigram is only air, it is not fire, water or earth; though its manifestation in matter is found in various things that operate under the aegis of air (traditionally, this includes the wind, plants/trees, and human intellect).

The Water trigram is only water, and not fire or earth or air; but it can be understood also as containing concepts like rivers, seas, lakes, marshes, swamps, as well as human joy/bliss and ecstatic emotion.

The Fire trigram is only fire, not water, air, or earth; but it also includes thunder, heat, movement, the fire under the earth, anything moving, consuming, arousing or exciting in humanity or in nature.

On the other hand, the celestial trigrams represent the full manifestation of each element in its dominant aspect over all other elements; in that way, we can envision each of the four celestial elements not only as a "bigger" or "stronger" version of their corresponding terrestrial element, but as encompassing all the terrestrial elements with one particular force ruling over them. Using the analogy of the western elemental pentagram, the celestial trigrams would each be the Invoking Pentagram of a particular element. When you draw an invoking pentagram of Water, you do not only draw water, you draw all the points of the pentagram from the perspective of Water; and likewise with each of the "Invoking Pentagrams".

Thus the Moon trigram contains within it aspects of Earth, Air, Water, and Fire, infused by spirit, and from the perspective of "invoking" Earth. In this way the Moon trigram represents the Moon; but also the idea of an abyss, a pit in the earth, the "great water" (in the sense of how the water is affected by the Moon in things like the tides or even the menstrual cycles of women), clouds, darkness, the night, the cold, danger, anything deep, and profound animal instinct in that sense of how animals (including human beings) are unconsciously affected by the patterns of the Moon.

The Sun trigram contains within it aspects of all four terrestrial elements, infused by spirit, and from the perspective of "invoking" the Air. The Sun is gas ignited by nuclear forces to create fire and heat and light. The Sun trigram also governs lightning and energy that is transmitted in non-material form. The Sun is brightness, elegance, brilliance as light shines down from the air. It is beauty; and illumination in the sense of that peak of what human intellect can achieve.

The World trigram contains within it all terrestrial elements (found in the world, obviously), infused by spirit, and from the perspective of "invoking" Water. Most of the world is covered by water, surrounded by water in the atmosphere, and full of water beneath its surface (as well as liquid fire). Thus The World trigram corresponds to heat, to darkness, to receptive forces; it is femininity, the Mother, the Yoni of the Tantrists, and it could in fact be called "the Universe" as it really encompasses the fullness of creation looking within itself; the downward-pointing triangle of the six-pointed star. It represents all that is open, receptive, devoted, and surrendering about human consciousness.

The Heaven Trigram has within it these same terrestrial elements, infused by spirit, and from the perspective of "invoking" Fire. It is the highest point to which the elements can aspire; the four elements and spirit united, the fullness of creation looking beyond itself. It is thus the upward-pointing triangle of the six-pointed star. Heaven is thus space infused with creative power. It is the sky (but also outer space), it is cold, but has energetic power. It is strength, the masculine, the Lingam of the Tantrists, the Father. In human consciousness it represents everything that aspires, that seeks to create, the Will seeking to act to overcome itself.

This understanding has enormous consequences in terms of "correspondences" with western esoteric symbolism and how the I Ching trigrams can be useful to the western practitioner. Just to begin with, it provides a whole new set of symbols that can be utilized to represent something not easily represented in symbolic form until now (the idea of an actively invoking elemental pentagram with a single pictogram). Beyond which, this has very big implications in terms of how a western practitioner can understand and contemplate both the western elemental system and the I Ching, enriching the understanding of both. It has further implications when you consider the relationship of the I Ching to the foremost divination system of the western tradition: the Tarot.

The Trigrams and Court Cards of the Tarot

Those of you who have even a basic level of study in western esoteric symbolism will likely have experience with the Tarot. And if you have studied the Tarot in the hermetic context, you may have already noted with some excitement how the elemental structure of the Trigrams has significant implications for creating direct correspondences between I Ching and the Tarot, in at least one area: the Court Cards of the Tarot's minor arcana.

The sixteen court cards each consist of a combination of two of the classical elements (or a single element doubled). There is thus a direct correspondence with the sixty four hexagrams of the I Ching, wherein each Court Card corresponds to four of the I Ching's hexagrams.

To give an example, the card known as the Knight of Disks in the Thoth tarot (known in other decks as the King of Coins or King of

Pentacles) is understood as the Fiery part of Earth. This would directly relate to the hexagram #62, "Small Gains" (Fire over Earth). Like the Knight of Disks, this hexagram advocates staying low, focusing on the necessities at hand and having small goals. You could also relate this card to the hexagram #33 "Retreat" (Heaven over Earth), which advocates withdrawal from large ambitions and again suggests that "you can persevere in small things, for gain". Likewise, you can relate the Knight of Disks to Hexagram #40, "Shooting" (Fire over Moon), which suggests "if there's no point in either staying put or charging forth, go back!" but that if you do have an actual point in taking action, you should do so with the utmost haste.Finally, it can relate to Hexagram #6 "Struggle" (Heaven over Moon), which suggests a time of difficulty and that taking things to extremes now foreshadows disaster.

You can similarly connect the various hexagrams to all of the court cards. The following lists the Court Card correspondences by number (with hexagrams listed for the upper and lower trigrams, respectively):

King/Knight of Wands: #51 (fire/fire), #25 (heaven/fire), #34 (fire/heaven), #1 (heaven/heaven);

Queen of Wands: #17 (water/fire), #24 (world/fire), #43 (water/heaven), #11 (world/heaven);

Prince of Wands: #42 (air/fire), #21 (sun/fire), #9 (air/heaven), #14 (sun/heaven);

Princess/page of Wands: #27 (earth/fire), #3 (moon/fire), #26 (earth/heaven), #5 (moon/heaven);

King/Knight of Cups: #54 (fire/water), #10 (heaven/water), #16 (fire/world), #12 (heaven/world);

Queen of Cups: #58 (water/water), #45 (world/water), #19 (water/world), #2 (world/world);

Prince of Cups: #61 (air/water), #38 (sun/water), #20 (air/world), #35 (sun/world);

Princess/Page of Cups: #41 (earth/water), #60 (moon/water), #23 (earth/world), #8 (moon/world);

King/Knight of Swords: #32 (fire/air), #44 (heaven/air), #55 (fire/sun), #13 (heaven/sun);

Queen of Swords: #28 (water/air), #46 (world/air), #49 (water/sun), #36 (world/sun);

Prince of Swords: #57 (air/air), #50 (sun/air), #37 (air/sun), #30 (sun/sun);

Princess/Page of swords: #18 (earth/air), #48 (moon/air), #22 (earth/sun), #63 (moon/sun);

Knight/King of Disks/coins: #62 (fire/earth), #33 (heaven/earth), #40 (fire/moon), #6 (heaven/moon);

Queen of Disks: #31 (water/earth), #15 (world/earth), #47 (water/moon), #7 (world/moon);

Prince of Disks: #53 (air/earth), #56 (sun/earth), #59 (air/moon), #64 (sun/moon);

Princess/Page of disks: #52 (earth/earth), #39 (moon/earth), #4 (earth/moon), #29 (moon/moon).

Thus we have the entirety of the I Ching reflected in the court cards of the tarot, in this particular group of correspondences. I have to note that in this particular model, on a personal level, I feel it reveals and instructs much more about the mysteries of the court cards than it illuminates new information about the I Ching.

The "Double Element" and "Big Element" Hexagrams

In the process of considering the elemental correspondences of the Trigrams there are two more details worthy of particular attention. These are the "double element" and "big element" hexagrams.

A "double-element" hexagram is simply any hexagram that consists of two of the same element. Thus #1 is the double-element hexagram of Heaven, #2 of The World, #30 of the Sun, #29 of the Moon, #51 of Fire, #58 of Water, #57 of Air, and #52 of Earth. These are significant because they are considered the most intense expression of one particular element; much in the same way that in the Tarot the Queen of Cups (water of water) is considered the most intense expression of the water element. By studying the double hexagram one can gain more insight into the trigram itself in its intensity. It is notable that these come in pairs: 1 and 2 (Heaven and World), 29 and 30 (Moon and Sun), 51 and 52 (Fire and Earth), 57 and 58 (Air and Water).

A "big element" hexagram is somewhat more unusual. In short, the "big element" hexagrams have to be imagined as a trigram of doubled lines. This means that each line in the trigrams is actually two in the hexagram. For example, let's say one wishes to find the "big element" trigram for the Air trigram:

As the Air trigram has one broken line followed by two solid lines, its "big element" hexagram would consist of two broken lines followed by four solid lines. Thus the "big element" hexagram would be #33 "Retreat":

Thus, Hexagram 33 looks like a "big" version of the Air Trigram.

It is important to note that in this case the hexagram's component trigrams do not in fact include air at all. Rather, they are Earth below and Heaven above. This is not always the case; "big Heaven" and "big World" are the same as "double Heaven" and "double World", in both cases hexagrams #1 and #2 respectively (but this is a feature of the special qualities of those two hexagrams). On the other hand, "big Sun" is Hexagram #61 (water below, air above), "big Moon" is Hexagram #62 (Earth below, Fire above), "big Fire" is Hexagram #19 (Water below, World above), "big Water" is Hexagam #34 (World below, Fire above), "big Earth" is Hexagram #20 (World below, Air above), and as described above "big Air" is Hexagram #33 (Earth below, Heaven above).

It is immediately notable that the "big hexagrams" (like the "double hexagrams") come in pairs: 1 and 2 (Heaven and World), 19 and 20 (Fire and Earth), 33 and 34 (Air and Water), and 61 and 62 (Sun and Moon).

While the "double hexagrams" unquestionably represent the direct elemental forces (at their fullest extension), the "big element hexagrams" are more speculative; they usually represent a more subtle manifestation of the elemental concept, since most of the hexagrams are not composed of the element in question at all. Heaven and The World, being the purest trigrams, are the exception to this; but in all other cases the hexagrams express the elemental energy at its most dispersed. For example, hexagram #19 as "big Fire", representing "Convergence (of Will)", relates to the quality of the Fire element as relating to Will, as the aspiration of terrestrial will to ascend and connect to the superior Will. "Big Earth", hexagram #20 ("Contemplating"), relates to Earth in the form of the Earth element's contemplative quality, of studying and understanding the mysteries of nature in order to ascend to Heaven's Virtue.

For this reason, contemplation of both the "double" and "big" hexagrams can lead the practitioner to new realizations as to the mysteries of the elements; in both the I Ching's internal context, and in the larger sense of how they relate to the esoteric tradition in East and West alike.

Planetary Correspondences

The elements are the most obvious correspondences for the (obviously elemental) trigrams of the I Ching. However, they are not the only correspondences that have been established. The correspondence between the trigrams and the planets of astrology is obviously of great interest to a western practitioner.

In western occultism, the planets correspond to the Tree of Life of the Qabalah; thus in establishing the correspondences between the trigrams and the planets we also take a significant step to mapping the I Ching system to the western esoteric tradition in general. The qualities of these correspondences are quite convincing. The placement of the trigrams on the Qabalistic Tree of Life will be explained in the following section, but even without having clear explanations of methodology, even a cursory glance of the correspondences as they relate to western imagery will make immediate sense to any individuals with some basic knowledge of astrological symbolism (whether or not they are familiar with the hermetic Qabalah). The correspondences are as follows:

Trigram	Planet
Heaven	Saturn
Water	Jupiter
Fire	Mars
Sun	Sun
Earth (element)	Venus
Air	Mercury
Moon	Moon
World	Earth

At first glance, some of these attributions might be confusing to those not familiar with either the Qabalah or the western astrological attributions. Saturn, the planet equivalent to Heaven, was the original lord of the heavens; and in the Qabalah it is the planet that represents the highest state, the level of reality beyond which creation itself ends. Jupiter is exalted in Cancer, the cardinal sign of Water; and the Water trigram in the I Ching represents the pleasant and complementary quality, reminiscent of Lao Tzu's Taoist teaching that "water is the supreme good", just as Jupiter was known as a great benevolent planet in western astrology. Mars is a fiery planet, and represents the exciting power of the Fire trigram. The correspondences for both the Sun and Moon trigrams are self-evident. The Earth Element trigram connects to Venus, a very physical planet, which includes the themes of sensuality in not only the romantic sense but also all forms of emotional engagement in the world; Venus rules Taurus, the most solid of the Earthly signs of the zodiac, and the Earth trigram has a strong correlation to the Taurus qualities of stubbornness, prudence, and simultaneously pleasurable engagement in the most basic of sensuality. The Air trigram is tied to Mercury, and that is not surprising at all, as Mercury symbolizes swift movement, intellect, the mind, and thought, all of which are deeply connected to the Air trigram concept. Finally, The World is clearly the Earth, the final receptive force of all other planetary influences.

The I Ching and the Qabalistic Tree of Life

Like the I Ching, the Qabalah is a system of cosmology; it tries to organize the nature of reality by ordering it according to stages, and through visual symbolism. The Qabalah originated as a Jewish mystical practice in the middle ages (evolving from earlier mystical practices in the Hebrew tradition), but the Qabalah as practised by most western magicians is not the same as the Hebrew Qabalah taught in orthodox Judaism or in trendy Hollywood "Qabalah Centres". It is instead termed the "Hermetic Qabalah" and dates to the fifteenth century when non-Jewish scholars, taking an interest in the study of Hebrew to better comprehend the Old Testament in its original language, came across the Qabalistic writings and were immediately entranced by their mysteries. These "Hermetic Qabalists" originally sought to use the Qabalah to find parallels or proofs of Christian doctrine in Hebrew mysticism, but from there the study evolved to a magical tool of extreme utility. The Qabalah, as they understood it, sought out the hidden connections between all things, and could thus be used in magick to understand the correspondences of all symbols. The Hermetic Qabalah evolved in its own direction on parallel lines with the Hebrew Qabalah so that while they began from the same sources, they became increasingly different from one another over the centuries.

The Hermetic Qabalah understands the system not as something contained within or limited to Hebrew scripture and dogma, but as a universal system, capable of expressing the nature of reality in a form separate from any particular religious expression of that reality. The Tree of Life, a fundamental symbol of the Qabalah, allows one to place any thing at all (any name, image, object, deity, number, sign, planet, spirit, scent, animal, plant, mineral, part of the body, or any other thing material or immaterial, or any idea or concept) on one of its ten spheres or twenty-two paths. This is very much the same idea as that expressed in the I Ching system, where Confucians confidently state that somewhere within the sixty-four hexagrams, eight trigrams, and the yin and yang or the Tai-ji (Tao), you can categorize any phenomenon in time or space.

It would take an entire book of its own to explain the full details of the Hermetic Qabalah (to those interested I would recommend the

Kether

1 Magician 0 Fool

Binah　　3 Empress　　**Chokhmah**

7 Chariot　6 Lovers　2 High Priestess　17 The Star　5 Hierophant

Geburah　　11 Strength　　**Chesed**

12 Hanged Man　8 Justice　9 Hermit　10 Wheel

Tiphareth

15 Devil　14 Temperance　13 Death

Hod　16 The Tower---- ---(Tower cont.)**Netzach**

19 The Sun　4 Emperor

Yesod

20 Judgment　21 The World　18 The Moon

Malkuth

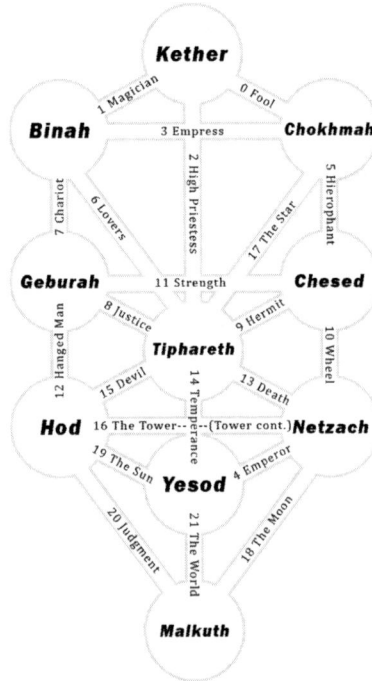

writings of Israel Regardie, Aleister Crowley, Dion Fortune, or Lon Milo Duquette); but for the purposes of the relationship between the Hermetic Qabalah and the I Ching, the main symbol that needs to be explained is the Qabalistic Tree of Life.

Above is an image of the Tree of life with its ten spheres and twenty-two paths. In this particular image of the Tree, the 22 paths are labelled according to the card of the Major Arcana of the Tarot that corresponds to each path; but each path similarly corresponds to one of the twenty-two letters of the Hebrew alphabet (as well as many other things).

The ten spheres ("sephira") represent ten different levels of reality; they also correspond to different planets, deities, and forces. The paths represent connections between one sphere and another, and thus concepts that unite one force to the other.

The expression of reality actually begins above the Tree of Life, with nothingness. This nothingness is called Ain (nothing), then Ain Soph (limitless), and finally Ain Soph Aur (the limitless light). All three of these are emptiness, but of different kinds; the latter is what in

Buddhism is called "luminous emptiness", a nothingness pregnant with potential. In the symbolism of the I Ching, this is equivalent to the "primordial Tao", Tao as Emptiness.

From this emptiness manifests absolute Oneness, a oneness so completely singular that it has no definition, there is no way to adequately define it. This is the sphere of Kether ("the crown"), the beginning of the Tree of Life. This is the Tao as Oneness, the Tao Tai Ji.

This Oneness, Kether, inherently contains within it the potential for duality. This duality manifests as the second and third spheres: Chokmah ("Wisdom") and Binah ("Understanding"), which are opposites to one another, masculine and feminine. At this level of reality, the singular point can now be definable by opposites, there is a theoretical form. Chokmah and Binah represent pure Yang and pure Yin.

Together, the first three spheres form a "Supernal Triad"; they are theoretical form, beyond all actual form. They are symbolically separated from the lower spheres by an Abyss, which is described as Daath, "Knowledge". It marks the furthest boundary of structural creation; and it is correspondent to Saturn. It is thus also correspondent to the Heaven trigram.

On the other side of the Abyss you find Chesed ("mercy") which adds structure; a triangle can now become a pyramid, you achieve solid form. Chesed corresponds to Jupiter and thus to the Water trigram. A fifth sphere, Geburah ("strength") adds the concept of movement, a sphere which can now operate in different co-ordinates over Time. This motion is represented by Mars, and the Fire trigram in the I Ching.

The sixth sphere, Tiphareth ("beauty") represents the return to the middle pillar, and the development of pure form into Consciousness. The matter that now has depth and motion (and thus exists in time) can now also be aware of itself. It corresponds to the Sun and thus to the Sun trigram.

Once Consciousness is manifest, it develops emotion and intellect; these are symbolized by the seventh and eighth spheres, Netzach ("victory") and Hod ("splendour"). They correspond to Venus and Mercury, and thus to the Earth and Air trigrams respectively.

These unite and emanate the ninth sphere, Yesod ("Foundation"). This is conception, creativity, the imagination, the archetypal world. It corresponds to the Moon, and thus to the Moon trigram.

Finally, the emanations of all the other levels descend into pure solid matter, our actual material world. This is Malkuth ("the kingdom"), it corresponds to the planet Earth and to The World trigram.

One important teaching found at the very core of the Qabalah is that "Kether is in Malkuth and Malkuth is in Kether". This means that, like the I Ching cosmology, the Tree of Life is cyclical. Although its image appears perhaps a bit more static than the changes obvious in the I Ching system, the Tree of Life is meant to represent a process of cycling; and indeed the system of divination most associated with it, the Tarot, is often referred to as a Wheel (the terms TARO and ROTA (wheel) being anagrams).

There is another important aspect to this teaching: it reveals that within each sphere, each concept contains within it the nature of all the other parts of the Tree. In the same way, we can understand that every trigram contains within it the essence of all the other trigrams in potentiality (as well as the Yin, the Yang, and the Tao itself). Similarly, every hexagram has the potentiality of every other hexagram within it, as is evident from the system for generating new hexagrams through changing lines. While some hexagrams are more likely to emerge from any given hexagram, in theory under the right conditions any hexagram may transform into any other hexagram in the future.

***

The correspondences of the hexagrams themselves to the I Ching are somewhat more in doubt. Much less work has been done to form a truly credible model. A number of approaches have been attempted, but each should be taken only as theoretical.

One clue that is immediately notable is the fact that the ten sephira plus the twenty-two paths make for thirty-two keyed "points" in the Tree of Life; one could thus assume that for each of these points you could fit two of the sixty-four hexagrams of the I Ching! Thus one postulated model for correspondences suggests simply putting the sixty four hexagrams, in order of the standard King Wen sequence, attributed two per point on the tree:

Hexagram Pair	Sphere/Path
1 & 2	Kether
3 & 4	Chokmah
5 & 6	Binah
7 & 8	Chesed
9 & 10	Geburah
11 & 12	Tiphareth
13 & 14	Netzach
15 & 16	Hod
17 & 18	Yesod
19 & 20	Malkuth
21 & 22	Aleph/Fool/Air
23 & 24	Beth/Magus/Mercury
25 & 26	Gimel/Moon/High Priestess
27 & 28	Daleth/Venus/Empress
29 & 30	Heh/Aquarius/Star
31 & 32	Vau/Taurus/Hierophant
33 & 34	Zain/Gemini/Lovers
35 & 36	Cheth/Cancer/Chariot
37 & 38	Teth/Leo/Lust
39 & 40	Yod/Virgo/Hermit
41 & 42	Kaph/Jupiter/Fortune
43 & 44	Lamed/Libra/Adjustment
45 & 46	Mem/Water/Hanged Man
47 & 48	Nun/Scorpio/Death
49 & 50	Samekh/Sagittarius/Art
51 & 52	Ayin/Capricorn/Devil

53 & 54	Peh/Mars/Tower
55 & 56	Tzaddi/Aries/Emperor
57 & 58	Qoph/Pisces/Moon
58 & 60	Resh/Sun/Sun
61 & 62	Shin/Fire/Aeon
63 & 64	Tau/Saturn/Universe

It seems that the only particular advantage of this approach to correspondence is its simplicity. Examined honestly, it appears to be an arbitrary superimposition of the King Wen sequence on a completely different way of ordering symbols, the Tree of Life. There is no particular reason why the process of organization of the Tree should be identical to those of the Hexagrams, as they begin with different underlying processes. Both seek to symbolically organize reality, but that does not mean they're going to do the organizing in the same way. If one were planning to take two library systems, where one was ordered alphabetically by title, and the other ordered according to year of publication, it would not work to just overlap them straight; there would be a need to adapt one to fit the other.

The logical course would seem to be to try to map the hexagrams to their corresponding places on the Tree of Life based on the planetary correspondences of the Trigrams. With all of these present on the Tree, this would be the most sensible course; but it immediately encounters a complication. While the I Ching allows for any combination of two forces, the Tree of Life does not allow for that in its image; there is no way to connect Water and Air directly, for example. Thus, through this method we face the possibility that while the entire Tree could be mapped to the I Ching system, the I Ching system is too detailed to be mapped in its entirety on the Tree of Life. Those areas that do have direct correspondences are as follows:

Sphere/Path	I Ching Hexagram
Kether	(Tao)
Chokmah	(Yang)
Binah	(Yin)
Chesed	58
Geburah	51
Tiphareth	30
Netzach	52
Hod	57
Yesod	29
Malkuth	2
Aleph/Fool/Air	(none) (possibly 9 and 44)
Beth/Magus/Mercury	(none) (possibly 9 and 44)
Gimel/Moon/High Priestess	1 (found in Daath)
Daleth/Venus/Empress	(none) (possibly lesser Yin/Yang*)
Heh/Aquarius/Star	13
Vau/Taurus/Hierophant	10 and 43
Zain/Gemini/Lovers	14
Cheth/Cancer/Chariot	25 and 34
Teth/Leo/Lust	17 and 54
Yod/Virgo/Hermit	38 and 49
Kaph/Jupiter/Fortune	31 and 41
Lamed/Libra/Adjustment	21 and 55
Mem/Water/Hanged Man	32 and 42
Nun/Scorpio/Death	22 and 56
Samekh/Sagittarius/Art	63 and 64
Ayin/Capricorn/Devil	37 and 50

Peh/Mars/Tower	18 and 53
Tzaddi/Aries/Emperor	4 and 39
Qoph/Pisces/Moon	15 and 23
Resh/Sun/Sun	48 and 59
Shin/Fire/Aeon	20 and 46
Tau/Saturn/Universe	7 and 8

*: These are the two-line combinations of one Yin and one Yang line. Likewise, the paths of Aleph and Beth may represent greater Yang and greater Yin respectively; these are two lines of both-solid or both-broken lines.

This system for correspondences leaves twenty hexagrams absent. Thus it is in no way fully satisfactory, and much speculation would need to follow in order to "fill in" where those remaining hexagrams would be assigned. We would have to presume, under this system, that in some way the hexagrams that are not directly expressible on the Tree of Life would have the following attributions:

Hexagram	*Attribution*
3	From Yesod to Geburah
5	From Yesod to Daath/Supernal Triad
6	From Daath/Supernal Triad to Yesod
9	From Hod to Daath/Supernal Triad
16	From Geburah to Malkuth
19	From Malkuth to Chesed
24	From Malkuth to Geburah
26	From Netzach to Daath/Supernal Triad
27	From Netzach to Geburah
28	From Chesed to Hod
33	From Daath/Supernal Triad to Netzach
35	From Tiphareth to Malkuth

36	From Malkuth to Tiphareth
40	From Geburah to Yesod
44	From Daath/Supernal Triad to Hod
45	From Chesed to Malkuth
47	From Chesed to Yesod
60	From Yesod to Chesed
61	From Hod to Chesed
62	From Geburah to Netzach

Finally, there are other possibilities to consider in mapping the I Ching to the western esoteric system. From the very origins of the Qabalah onward, there have been alternate models or depictions of the Tree of Life. For example, the Sefer Yetzirah (one of the oldest qabalistic texts) presents a circular Tree of Life; this is repeated in the writings of the profoundly influential Hermetic Order of the Golden Dawn (a group that was deeply formative to Aleister Crowley at the beginning of his magical career), where the Golden Dawn material speculated on a model for the Tree of Life presented as a three-dimensional sphere (the model was used primarily to map the tree of life against the Zodiac, but there's no reason a similar model could not be attempted to map the Tree of Life to the cosmology of the I Ching).

Another possible model is the Cube of Space. This is a model mapping the Hebrew Alphabet (and mysteries of the Qabalah) to a cubic form. It too has its origins in the Sefer Yetzirah, and in the twentieth century was greatly developed for the Hermetic Qabalah by Paul Foster Case (among others).

On a final note, it cannot be discounted that there may be ways to obtain correspondences between the Tarot (which is thoroughly correspondent to the Tree of Life) and the Tree itself. The groundwork is already in the tables above. Mapping seventy eight cards to sixty four hexagrams may seem a challenge, but a possible key could be in the adding together of the hexagrams, the eight trigrams, the four two-line forms (the "greater and lesser Yin and Yang"), and the two single-line Yin and Yang forms. You thus end up with seventy eight entries, which could theoretically be mapped to the seventy eight cards of the Tarot.

Yi-Fa as a Magical Word and Current

Chapter One of this book explained the context of the term "Yi-Fa", the "manifested state", as "the Law of Change". It is my position that this concept should be seen as a keystone to understanding the relationship between the I Ching and esoteric practice, as well as the way to comprehend the I Ching's function in measuring space and time. It is an important concept because it creates context for how the I Ching should be approached as a divination practice; but more importantly, how the I Ching can be used as a sophisticated guidebook for magical philosophy. It relates the I Ching in a fundamental fashion to western occultism and particularly to the philosophical implications of Thelema.

While in the first chapter I approached this word in its original context of Confucian history, here I would like to examine it as a magical word and current, to describe in archetypal terms its "force" as a governing principle of the I Ching. And its magical levels and implications are profound.

If we were to examine the "Hermetic Qabalah" of "Yi-Fa" we could explore the word as "II VH", which by gematria (qabalistic numerology) corresponds to the number thirty-one, a key number in Thelemic practice. This ties it to the Thelemic current, and to the Book of the Law. The number thirty-one corresponds to "AL" ("god", "everything") as well as "LA" ("emptiness", "not"). It also corresponds to "HVK" (the verb "to go"), which implies the moveable quality of the I Ching and the entire philosophy of the "Law of Change".

"Yi-Fa" can be understood as the "Way of Change"; "way" in the sense of both a path, and also as a method. It is where you are going and what you are doing, all at once. It is both what you must embody, and where you must approach.

Visually, "II" implies an empty space between boundaries. It can be thought of as the twin pillars that frame the Qabalistic Tree of Life; or likewise the black and white columns found on either side of several cards of the Tarot, particularly the High Priestess, guardian of the mysteries. These evolve into the two towers that mark the borders in the Moon card.

VH, on the other hand, can be seen as the path between these pillars/towers; for as "II"/Yi is the polarity of "change", "VH"/Fa is the constancy of "the way". In the Moon trump, this path is the path toward the Sun (the subsequent card), and stylistically the "V" implies this deep valley, the cliff one falls from the Tower of false stability, into the deep waters of the unconscious (seen at the very bottom of the Moon card). The path emerges from this, it creates a bridge between the dark of the deep subconsciousness and the light of the higher self or "True Will". The letter "H" stylistically resembles a bridge between the two towers of "II"; the visible path that brings one into the garden of the Sun.

In all this mystical symbolism, it is important to remember that the key of any path, of the verb "to go", is to actually move, and take action in the world. Fundamentally, the Yi-Fa is not something to merely speculate upon, but to live through regular and steady practice and progress.

I should note that none of this is conventional to I Ching academia, much less to typical fortune-tellers. This is my own manifesto. No attempt is being made to bow here to either academic or Confucian orthodoxy; I present this as something inspired by the works of Zhu Xi, but this is my own declaration. It is the product of my attainment.

Chapter Five

The Shao Yung "Plum Blossom Method" of I Ching Numerology

As explained in the first chapter, Shao Yung was one of the great innovators in the practice of the I Ching; he could almost certainly be considered the most significant figure in I Ching studies outside of those nearly legendary figures that are credited with forming the very canon of the I Ching (Fu Xi, King Wen, and Confucius). He was notable as an outsider from the institutional mainstream (as indeed Confucius himself was in his own times), and for being a great defender of the necessity of actual use of the I Ching as a divination system and system of practice, rather than just a document for intellectual study (once again, a view that was largely in opposition to the conventional wisdom of the intelligentsia of his own age; and likewise paralleled Confucius' own views and situation in his own life).

Shao Yung was responsible for many innovations or discoveries in I Ching studies. He was almost certainly the one truly responsible for conceiving of the "early heaven" directional model for the trigrams, even though it was attributed to Fu Xi; he was likewise the most instrumental in elucidating the nature of the I Ching as a system of binary code. But most importantly, he designed (or, if the legend is to be believed, received from a mysterious "old sage" which may in fact have been an allegory for his own higher self) an entirely novel system of I Ching divination. Because the key of how to apply this method was discovered while observing a plum tree, it is called the "Plum Blossom" (or sometimes "plum flower") method.

There are several unique and interesting features to this system: in the first place, it is not a standard "divination" method because it does not rely on a (seemingly) random generation of a hexagram (in the way that casting staves, yarrow stalks, or coins do). Instead, it is based on a series of mathematical calculations, or alternately on the intuitive observation of nature. In this sense, it is in some ways more similar to Astrology than to generating systems like the Tarot, Runes, or the standard methods of I Ching castings. It is most accurately described as a system of temporal numerology, because in its most fundamental form it derives a hexagram through the analysis of dates and times. This also means that the Plum Blossom system is ideal for careful predictive forecasts based on determining dates and times.   It can thus be used to examine the process of events starting from specific moments, to obtain a "natal hexagram" of the date and time of your birth, or for judging the "auspiciousness" of particular dates with relation to particular activities.

While there have been a handful of books published that detail the Plum Blossom method (or at least make reference to it), on the whole this is one area of I Ching studies that has been underdeveloped in the west. In part because it has only been in the last couple of decades that western students of the I Ching have really moved beyond the most fundamental core part of the I Ching canon in terms of studies; and the Plum Blossom method is certainly not a part of the traditional Canon of the I Ching. There is also a further problem involved with the Plum Blossom method: it depends largely on the use of the Chinese calendar. This means that to be used properly, a western date needs to be converted into its correct numerical equivalents in the Chinese (lunar) calendar, a calendar which changes in relative position to the western calendar every year.

For some writers, the "solution" to this problem was simply to ignore the situation, and present the method using western dates and times. But this ignores the significance of the system as relating to geomantic and astrological concepts. As a mere fortune-telling oracle, it would likely still have value (in the same sense that you could tell someone that a tarot card can "just mean whatever you feel like it means"); but then why bother with the rest of the method at all? One might as well take this approach to its logical conclusion and simply tell practitioners to pick any two trigrams their intuition leads them to pick (and once again, there can be a certain value to that). Fortunately, the advent of the internet has continued to simplify matters for practitioners of all kinds of magical practices in terms of obtaining information, and Chinese Calendar conversions are no exception. It is now easier than it ever was before in the west to quickly convert the dates correctly, as the material below will explain, and thus the one real barrier to using the Plum Blossom method in its full context has now been overcome.

Before proceeding, it should be noted that there are many different presentations of "Plum Blossom method" I Ching that vary considerably in their methodology. What will be presented here is not exclusive or definitive, but it is what I believe to be both the core of the system as well as the most useful part. Because the Plum Blossom method was less supported by Confucian orthodoxy, and was conversely widely embraced by professional fortune tellers (part of its appeal was that it laid less reliance on the I Ching as a book; some go so far as to create variant methods that don't use the actual text of the I Ching at all!), there is far more diversity of methods.

The first step to generating a Plum Blossom method hexagram is to figure out a way to relate a value to the theme of the reading: the ideal is to be able to tie the reading to a particular date. This could be, for example, the birth date of the person in question, if what you are aiming for is an "astrology chart"-style overall analysis of the person and the course of his life. Other possibilities would include significant dates and times related to the issue. It is not enough to simply use the present date and time, unless the issue in question is one that requires immediate resolution (at this date, and at this very time). Questions that are most suited for a Plum Blossom method reading (as opposed to a standard I Ching casting) are enquiries such as: "would x time be the right moment to start this new project?"; "should I quit x on such-and-such date?"; "what will be the broad issues related to the lifespan of a person born on x date?"; "what are the broad and general events and issues related to a period of time beginning on date x?", etc.

As the information below will explain, it is also possible to engage in comparative readings, where one might look at the "compatibility" between two dates. For example, to compare the birth date of a person to the current date in order to see if the overall situation is favourable or inauspicious for them, or to compare the birth dates of two people to judge if one person will be "compatible" with the other. Finally, if the issue cannot reasonably be connected to a particular date at all, the mechanics of the Plum Blossom method could still be explored through the combination of an exploration of the present time to generate one trigram and an intuitive "augury" of some significant characteristic of the issue to generate the other component trigram.

To generate a hexagram through the standard Plum Blossom method, you must calculate the number values of the hour, day, month, and year based on the Chinese calendar.

Number values for the hour are determined by the following method:

Western Hour	*Hour Value*
11pm-1am	1
1am-3am	2
3am-5am	3
5am-7am	4
7am-9am	5
9am-11am	6
11am-1pm	7
1pm-3pm	8
3pm-5pm	9
5pm-7pm	10
7pm-9pm	11
9pm-11pm	12

Note that for a "birth chart" it is necessary to know the subject's hour of birth within a two-hour range; without it, one cannot use the standard method to generate a hexagram. This is unfortunate for those who do not have this information, but it is too crucial a part of the generation method to be avoidable. Aside from replacing the numerical method of generation with the more "intuitive" method (which I feel is particularly unsuitable for a "natal chart" type of reading), the only other advice which could really be offered to someone in this situation is to try to generate a hexagram based on some other date (where the time is also known) relevant to the subject the individual is most interested in learning about.

The day, month, and year are all based on the Chinese Lunar Calendar. The year's number value is easy enough to generate, as it is keyed to the Chinese Zodiac (which has by now become a common cultural detail in the West):

Chinese Zodiac Year:	Number Value:
Rat	1
Ox	2
Tiger	3
Rabbit/Hare	4
Dragon	5
Snake	6
Horse	7
Goat/Sheep	8
Monkey	9
Rooster	10
Dog	11
Boar/Pig	12

Western years correspond to the Chinese Zodiac Year around the first two months of the year; the precise date of the Chinese New Year varies from year to year (due to the use of the Lunar calendar with occasional "leap months"); so the Chinese New Year can happen any time between early January and late February. Most of 2014 (from 31 January) corresponds to the year of the Horse; 2015 (from 19 February) to the year of the Goat, 2016 (from 8 February) to the year of the Monkey, etc. Similarly, 2013 was the year of the Snake, 2012 the year of the Dragon, 2011 the year of the Rabbit, and so on.

The "Month" number values are thus the lunar months starting from the Chinese new year, and do not precisely correspond to western months, although very rough approximations can be attempted based on the information above. The date is based on the twenty-nine or thirty day-long months of the lunar calendar. For example, as the year of the Horse began on 31 January 2014, the western date of 26 February 2014 would be the twenty-seventh day of the first month of the seventh (horse) year.

Clearly, it would be very complicated if one had to resort to trying to calculate the Chinese calendar date from scratch. Similarly, if having to learn Chinese in order to read a Chinese calendar were necessary, the Plum Blossom method would be inaccessible to most westerners. Fortunately, neither of these are required in this day and age; the internet has several sources for conversions that make the whole process relatively painless. One of the best of these as of the time of this writing is the website of the Hong Kong observatory, which lists conversion charts from 1901-2100:

http://www.hko.gov.hk/gts/time/conversion1_text.htm

Once you have acquired the relevant number values you can generate the component trigrams. To generate the lower trigram you would need to add the number values of the hour, day, month and year, then divide this total by eight. The resulting remainder (note: the remainder, not a decimal value) will produce a trigram:

Remainder	Trigram
1	Heaven
2	Water
3	Sun
4	Fire
5	Air
6	Moon
7	Earth
8 (0)	World

For example, if we were to use the date above of 26 February, 2014, with the time of 10:30am, we would end up adding the following number values:

1(month) + 27 (day) + 7 (year) + 6 (hour) = 41

Divided by eight we generate $41/8 = 5$, with a remainder of 1 (as 8 x 5 = 40, and 41 – 40 = 1). Observing the list of Trigrams we see that 1 equals the Heaven trigram.

To generate the upper trigram, we would add the day, month, and year values (without the hour), then likewise divide by eight and use the remainder to obtain the trigram. In the above example we would thus have:

1(month) + 27 (day) + 7 (year) = 35

35 / 8 = 4, with a remainder of 3

From the list of Trigrams we see that 3 equals the Sun trigram. Thus our complete hexagram is #14, Great Holdings, Sun over Heaven:

In most cases of operating with the Plum Blossom method we will also want to generate a changing line (in this method, only a single changing line is ever used). To generate the changing line, we would use the same number values as for the lower trigram (time, month, day, and year), but in this case divide by six rather than eight; the resulting remainder (with remainder 0 counting as "6") would indicate the changing line. Note that, as before, you could generate the changing line by some intuitive or alternative method instead (for example, dividing the hour of the subject, or even of the actual reading, into six ten-minute parcels and using that number of the time as the changing line number, or looking for a number value in your surroundings, between one and six, to designate for the changing line). Some mathematicians have pointed out that by using the same value for the lower trigram as for the changing line (as Shao Yung's method does), this will end up excluding the possibilities of certain changing lines ever being selected for certain hexagrams; and have then suggested various alternate methods for correcting this "anomaly". However, given Shao Yung's obvious mathematical knowledge, it seems unlikely he wouldn't have been well aware of this situation himself and must have considered it a feature, rather than a "bug" of his methods. Although this method's anomaly seems problematic, I think it would be naive to simply jump to find some other simplified solution. While it is something that I have been considering for some time now, even in the many years I have studied, I do not yet feel qualified to claim that any other method would actually be more accurate. Thus I present to you the system as Shao Yung did it.

In this case, the month, day, year and hour values adding to 41, we have:

41 / 6 = 6, with a remainder of 5. Thus the fifth line is the changing line of this particular reading. This generates our future hexagram, which in this case happens to be #1, Creation:

In the Plum Blossom method it is also considered of great importance to observe the nuclear hexagram, as it reflects the inner or hidden qualities of the situation (not of the individual in question, note, but the situation itself). The nuclear hexagram is generated by the usual fashion. In our example, combining the second, third, and fourth lines of Hexagram #14 we get the Heaven trigram; and combining the third, fourth, and fifth lines of the hexagram we get the Water trigram. Thus the Nuclear Hexagram is #43, "Resolve":

These are the three hexagrams used in a Plum Blossom method reading.

After generating the hexagrams, the next step is to determine the "subject" trigram. The "subject" trigram (called "Ti" in Chinese) is the source of the reading; in the case of the reading being about a person, it represents the core of that person (likewise if the reading is about an object it represents that object, or situation, etc.). The "subject" trigram is always the trigram of the original hexagram that does NOT contain the moving line. In our example, with Hexagram #14, as the changing line is line 5 (thus, in the upper trigram), the "subject" trigram is the lower trigram, Heaven. All of the other trigrams of the reading are viewed relative to this one, and are called "fate" trigrams. The fate trigrams (originally called "Yong") are the representation of the different environments or forces acting upon the subject. These are going to be of paramount importance, and are the great innovation of the Plum Blossom method; where the trigrams are compared to one another according to their compatibility to determine the details of auspiciousness or in-auspiciousness in the situation. It is by examining how the elemental trigrams interact with one another that detailed interpretations are laid out.

First, however, one should review the images of each hexagram, considering carefully what those images elicit in one's mind. Just as Shao Yung developed the real practical key of this method while observing a plum blossom tree, this method is one that demands a certain kind of contemplative trance-state. More so than the regular I Ching method, the Plum Blossom method requires that the users turn off their minds just a little, and allow the image and lines of the hexagrams, of the elemental trigrams, of the scenes they create, to evoke concepts and insights in the readers' consciousness. In some cases, as with the story of Shao Yung and his son trying to determine what their neighbour's visit was about, just consideration and contemplation on the component trigrams may reveal an answer (and just like in that story, whether you can accurately guess that answer will depend on a combination of your experience in divination practice, and your consideration and awareness of the nature of things at this very moment). Shao Yung made it very plain that if you do not pause, contemplate, observe nature at the moment, and tie all this into your operation, you are bound to make mistakes.

Beyond this contemplation, one should also review the main text and especially the changing line oracle of the hexagram; as well as the image and main texts of the nuclear and resulting "future" hexagram. In some schools of Plum Blossom I Ching, this is almost entirely skipped; a few schools teach only to look at the one changing line, a few ignore even that and focus only on image and the interaction of elements, without referring to the actual text of the I Ching at all! This, however, seems to be a step too far born out of the less rigorous "fortune telling" practices of the Chinese equivalent of street-psychics, wary of Confucian intellectualism, and wishing only to rely on their own "psychic insights" without any inconvenient framework to oblige any kind of rigour or discipline. In my own experience, at least, the study of the main text and line oracle remain absolutely central to the practice of the Plum Blossom method.

This achieved, we now additionally obtain information based on the comparison of the elemental qualities (information that, in my experience, must be interpreted within this context of the hexagram meanings and changing lines). The elements are compared to each other, and follow set rules by which certain elements generate others, certain elements strengthen others, some clash with others, some drain or reduce others, and some eliminate others. These relationships are based on the relation of the elemental trigrams to the "Wu Xing", the Five Phases.

In some books the Wu Xing is translated as the "five elements", as they appear to also be an elemental system, with the names of wood, fire, earth, metal, and water. However, these are neither terrestrial nor celestial elements in the sense of the I Ching trigrams. They most closely correspond to states of growth and decline similar to the three Gunas of Indian occultism or the three Alchemical Elements (salt, sulphur, mercury) of western occultism. They describe phases of transition.

The five phases have been popularized and bastardized to the point that, in modern uses in both East and West (in things like mundane Feng Shui) there is very little understanding of their ancient meaning. In the oldest surviving texts where they are discussed it is very clear that these Phases do not describe states of matter, but of "Virtues", powers, they are ways of tracking states of change. In these oldest texts, they were most often compared to the course of the seasons in nature; they mainly deal with cycles and processes.

It is (fortunately) not essential to really understand the mysteries of the Five Phases in order to use the Plum Blossom method, but for those who want to understand the underlying principles of the method, it should be noted that the rules for how trigrams interact with one another are based upon the relationship these trigrams have with the Five Phases.

The Phases are:

1. "Wood"/Spring/Generation: the start of growth

2. "Fire"/Summer/Flowering: the peak of growth, the solstice.

3. "Earth"/Late Summer/Plateau: the period of prolonged stability

4. "Metal"/Fall/Decline: the period where process is deteriorating.

5. "Water"/Winter/Barrenness: the absolute bottom of the process, winter solstice, movement has stopped (until, naturally, spring begins the phases anew).

The Eight Trigrams are connected to these Phases as follows:

1. Generation: Fire and Air.

2. Flowering: Sun

3. Plateau: Earth and The World

4. Decline: Heaven and Water

5. Barrenness: Moon

There is great elegance in these correspondences. It is interesting to note that two solstices have only one trigram associated with them, expressing their relatively fleeting nature (the absolute peak or the absolute nadir are both states that are inherently temporary). It is also interesting to note that (contrary to the traditional Confucian relationships) in this Shao Yung set of correspondences, the trigrams corresponding to "generation" are those elements traditionally considered "masculine" in the West, while those connected to "decline" are the western "feminine" elements. The positioning of Heaven as "decline" might seem somewhat odd, but when you have a force of such strength it can only possibly decline from there. The Heaven trigram in this model could only be thought of as an "Indian summer", a last hurrah of force that is in fact predictive of things beginning to fall apart (it conjures images of some late attempt at reform or return to glory after a long period of stagnation).

Fate Trigram

Subject	Fire ⚏	Air ☴	Sun ⚏	Earth ☷	World ⚏	Heaven ☰	Water ⚏	Moon ☷
Fire ⚎	S	S	R	C	C	E	E	G
Air ☴	S	S	R	C	C	E	E	G
Sun ⚏	G	G	S	R	R	C	C	E
Earth ☷	E	E	G	S	S	R	R	C
World ☷	E	E	G	S	S	R	R	C
Heaven ☰	C	C	E	G	G	S	S	R
Water ☵	C	C	E	G	G	S	S	R
Moon ☷	C	C	E	G	G	S	S	R

To determine how any elemental trigram interacts with any other, consult the table above.

Explanation of Codes

S: These fate trigrams strengthen the subject. The situation is positive and easy at this stage; the subject and the situation are in mutual accord.

R: These fate trigrams reduce the subject. The situation is inauspicious, and only considerable effort, discipline, and hard work can prevail here. The subject has the potential to be in command over the situation.

C: These fate trigrams clash with the subject. The situation is tumultuous, but this too can be auspicious. It is important to be very careful, because it is easy for fortune to be disrupted. It is necessary to move carefully, and take advantage of change without bringing on unnecessary conflict or opposition. The subject must take command of the situation.

E: These fate trigrams eliminate the subject. The situation is highly inauspicious at this stage. It is only mitigated by judicious application of virtue, and careful conservative choices. The situation overwhelms the subject; it is beyond the subject's control.

G: These fate trigrams generate the subject. The situation has the potential to be very auspicious, if the subject is willing to move along with it. The situation is beyond the subject's control; but if the subject accords to the reality of the situation, the result is positive.

To continue to apply our example of determining an augury for some process related to the date 26 February, 2014 (at 10:30am): we had, at this point, generated Hexagram #14 as our base hexagram, with #43 as its nuclear hexagram and (with changing line 5) leading to hexagram #1 as the future hexagram. The imagery of hexagram #14 (Great Holdings) is of the Sun in splendour, the core message is of "riches and virtue", and line 5 says: "In society he is sincere and confident, earning respect. Dignity is the greatest wealth. Good fortune! (He is poor, but rich in dignity, honest and bold in demeanour, and thus wins great regard)". This forms the central oracle, indicating that in spite of material difficulty, other qualities can allow us to succeed.

The Nuclear hexagram, "Resolve", portrays the imagery of a lake evaporating into the sky. The main text warns about the risk of being too honest, and the importance of getting help from other sincere people; these messages should be seen as underlying the message of the main hexagram.

The future hexagram, "Creation", contains the image of the four Confucian virtues: "Sublime celestial forces in motion" (Love, Right Conduct, Justice, and Wisdom). This is in continuity with the message of the main hexagram (of demonstrating virtues to win regard). The promise of the future hexagram text is that if one maintains a right course, reward will be the result. It is already evident that the general reading is very positive as to the events related to this date.

The subject trigram of this reading is the Heaven trigram, the lower of the two trigrams in hexagram #14, because it is the trigram that does not have a changing line. To look at the interactions of the trigrams, we would begin by comparing Heaven to the upper trigram, the Sun. Referring to the table above, we see that the Sun trigram "eliminates" the Heaven trigram, implying a very problematic situation where little can be done and that is outside the Subject's control to avoid. This may be the cause for the initial consultation, and may relate to line 5 of the hexagram; if the reader was not told the motive for the reading, he might surmise that the subject finds himself in a situation where for reasons not of his own doing he is in serious material difficulty and trying to find out how to change his situation for the better.

The lower trigram of the nuclear hexagram is Heaven, and this matches and thus "strengthens" the subject. Furthermore, the upper Water trigram, being representative of the same "phase", likewise strengthens the subject. Heaven and Water are both of the phase of decline; an analysis of the trigrams from the perspectives of the five phases would thus suggest that the present situation is one where the problem is at its peak (symbolized by the Sun hexagram, which belongs to the "flowering" phase), and now the crisis that has brought about the current problem is in a state of decline. The initial period will be very difficult, as all the subject has to rely upon are his personal virtues, but this will be enough. The problem will begin to evaporate under the power of Heaven's virtue (much like the imagery of a lake evaporating into the sky in the nuclear hexagram); and assistance from others that admire the subject's virtue will lead into a prolonged period of strengthening. This is confirmed by the two "strengthening" Heaven trigrams in the future hexagram, where keeping the right course results in reward.

Summary of the Plum Blossom Method Standard Procedure

1. Calculate number values for date, time, month, and year, converted from the Chinese Lunar Calendar.

2. Calculate lower trigram of main hexagram by adding values for:

Hour + Day + Month + Year

then divide by 8 and use the remainder to determine the trigram.

3. Calculate upper trigram of main hexagram by adding values for:

Day + Month + Year

then divide by 8 and use the remainder to determine the trigram.

4. Calculate the changing line of the hexagram by adding the values for:

Hour + Day + Month + Year

then divide by 6, and the remainder is the line that is changing (a result with no remainder means line 6 is the changing line).

5. Generate the Future hexagram in the standard fashion.

6. Generate the Nuclear hexagram in the standard fashion.

7. Study the image of the hexagram, as well as the main text description, and the changing line oracle.

8. Study the images and main texts of the Nuclear hexagram and the Future hexagram. Contemplate all of the above carefully.

9. In the main hexagram, the "Subject" trigram is the trigram that does not contain a changing line. Compare this trigram to each other trigram in turn on the list of elemental compatibilities; beginning with the other main hexagram trigram to determine the overall current situation, then with the lower and upper nuclear trigrams to determine the other influences upon the situation, and finally the two trigrams of the future hexagram to determine future developments of the situation.

There are a few other details and tricks to consider in the "Plum Blossom" method of I Ching numerology:

Other ways of generating trigrams: If we cannot use time values, several schools of Shao Yung's method also make use of certain alternative methods. Probably the most common (and one that records show Shao Yung himself used) is to calmly observe one's surroundings at the time of preparing the hexagram. The idea is to look for hints in these surroundings as to imagery that will relate to one of the Trigrams. Some of these will be very literal: if one's attention is drawn to a lit candle in front of one's eyes, for example, that would indicate the Fire trigram. Feeling a soft breeze or draft might indicate the Air trigram. On the other hand, this observation practice might also be less literal and instead form from a process of intuitive connections; for example, one might hear music playing and associate that with the Air element.Seeing something bright blue might bring the Water element to mind. Some empty curved object (a bowl, for example) might conjure up the image of the Moon trigram.

This method can potentially be very fruitful; however it relies on having a very trustworthy sense of intuition. The "changing line" in this case can be derived from some numerical cue in the environment (noticing four pieces of cutlery on the table in front of you, for example, may lead you to conclude that the changing line is line 4). A very useful alternate method would be to consider some symbol related to the subject of the reading; for example, if someone had been worried about possibly losing his cellphone, the quality of the cellphone itself might suggest the Heaven trigram to you (although its nature as a communication device could just as easily suggest the Air trigram; this is the difficulty of this method).

Another very common method used by many Chinese Plum Blossom readers is to generate a numerical value based on a word or name. This is done by counting the number of brush-strokes required to draw the ideogram of the word; dividing this by eight, and obtaining a remainder (as with the date-focused method above) in order to find the hexagram. For example, if a word required five brushstrokes, it would correspond to the Air trigram; if a name required thirteen brushstrokes in total, it would also correspond to the Air trigram (because 13/8 = 1, with 5 remainder). This method does not automatically translate to the West, since western words use letters rather than ideograms. It would be theoretically possible instead to assign number values based on the number of pen-strokes required to write a word, but clearly this is not quite the same. A few writers have suggested instead that one could use a numerological value where one would add the simple number-order value of a letter (ie. A=1, B=2, C=3, etc). This last idea opens up an interesting possibility for the Qabalist; if one used qabalistic gematria (the art of calculating a number value of a word by using the numerical values of the Hebrew alphabet), this method could suggest that any gematric number would have a trigram associated with it. For example, the number 93 would correspond to the Air trigram (as 93/8 = 11, with 5 remainder). The Hebrew word Achad ("unity") numerates to 13, thus it too would have the Air trigram as its element.

Calculating time scales using the Plum Blossom method: One of the aspects of the Plum Blossom method, perhaps due to its popularity among the more pragmatic fortune-tellers of Chinese culture, is the focus on trying to make precise measurements of time scales. In China, fortune tellers are expected to give very precise and accurate measurements, not vague predictions; they are also usually consulted for very concrete questions regarding practical and material concerns; being far less concerned with "psychological" matters, and much more concerned with questions about issues like specific work goals, marriage, children, investments, construction, and so on. All of these demand some kind of relatively precise temporal prediction.

As before, there are a variety of schools of thought about how to judge time-scales according to the Plum Blossom method; in fact, there may be dozens of different ideas. And of course, the nature of the time-span of the question affects how one might scale the answer: a question regarding events that could take years to unfold will require a different time-scale than those that require months, or weeks, or days.

In terms of what are perhaps the most significant keys to the relationship between time-measurement and the Plum Blossom system, there are two specific attributions that are the most useful. The first relates to the six lines of the hexagram. As with the standard I Ching system, it is understood that from bottom to top, these lines represent progressive developments; so clearly time flows from the lower line up to the top line, with the lowest line representing the oldest force (that which is starting to pass away into history) and the highest sixth line representing the newest influence. Thus, in the Plum Blossom numerological system, these six lines are also taken to represent six divisions in the flow of time. In some interpretations, they can represent a six-month period, for example, with one line per month. In this way, the main hexagram and future hexagram's component lines can be thought of as covering a full year period. It should be noted that the line interpretations in the core text are not usually referred to in this context; instead, the trigrams are considered (and the elemental compatibility that is being experienced at that time), as well as whether the line is Yin or Yang, and whether it is in a good position for its line (for example, a solid line is well-dignified if it is in the first, third, or fifth place; while it would be ill-dignified in the second, fourth or sixth place; and the inverse applies to the broken lines). Likewise, the overall situation of the lines are considered (for example, a broken line even in the third or fifth place can be considered positive, or at least less negative, if it is surrounded by strong solid lines supporting it both above and below).

The other significant standard for the measurement of time in Plum Blossom numerology is in the value of the lines. Yin lines (broken lines) are valued at 6, while yang lines (solid lines) are valued at 9. These two numbers can be used to represent any number of time measurements: hours, days, weeks, months, years or more. In "natal chart" styles of Plum Blossom readings, the age or duration of long term periods can be predicted by calculating the lines, from the bottom up, as values of 6 or 9. This is used especially in determining the "key period" of the changing line.

In the "natal chart", the changing line is considered to be the absolute most significant or crucial period of the subject's life, the part that will be most defining. The date and age-range of this period can be determined by this counting method. For example, in our sample reading above (Hexagram #14), if we were to assume it was a "natal chart" for a person born on 26 February, 2014 (10:30 am), the changing fifth line would indicate that the most crucial period of a person's life would begin at age thirty seven and last until age forty two. This is because you have four Yang lines below it (so 9 x 4 = 36) and the changing line itself is a Yin line (and thus lasts six years).

Clearly, a tremendous amount of intuition has to be applied in the use of these types of calculations, as there is no hard and fast rule as to when or how to apply them. The context of the reading, and the intuition of the reader, must be used to determine just what kind of time scales these numbers refer to.

It is also worth repeating that these are not the only methods used. The relative lack of "authoritative" rules in Plum Blossom practice is due to the fact that while the I Ching's canon has been studied, governed and regulated to a certain extent by the Chinese Confucian "Academia" of the last two thousand years, establishing concepts of what is orthodox and what is not, Shao Yung's system was decidedly unorthodox. While greatly respected in Chinese society, Shao Yung was always a rebel and an outsider; he never held significant offices, and his focus was on the use of the I Ching for divination, something that the Confucian mainstream denigrated (except those who were the most wise and learned of the Confucians, all of whom ironically advocated the practice of divination). Thus, the Plum Blossom system became a method largely given over to the diviners and the fortune-tellers; the intellectual underclass who were not under any central authority. Only time, tradition, and personal experiences of what actually works allowed for certain methods to win out over certain others.

To give just two other examples when it comes to time scales, that are somewhat less reliable but may be of use: first, one can use the main hexagram to predict a time scale within a 24 hour period. To do this, look up the number associated with the two hexagrams (for example, Heaven is 1, Fire is 4, The World is 8, etc.) Add these together, and add them to the number of the changing line. This gives you a period in hours. In our example with Hexagram 14, we have Heaven (1) + Sun (3) + line (5), meaning that the total period covered is nine hours long.

Second, another way to predict a longer time scale would be to take the number of the lower trigram, multiply it by ten, and then add it to the number of the higher trigram and the changing line. So if we used this method to predict a span of time with Hexagram #14, we have (1 x 10) + 3 + 5 = 18. Hopefully this would not be used to predict a life expectancy!

In my own opinion, these two methods seem more arbitrary and generate less reliable results than the former two time scale methods described above. But I include them as an example that the Plum Blossom Method is a source of constant experimentation; while it follows certain hard rules, it has constantly been modified and innovated in ways that the more orthodox I Ching canonical material no longer experiences. This continues to this day, where new writers have presented novel ideas for Plum Blossom numerology, including attempts to convert the system so that it is simplified for modern Chinese practitioners as well as westerners. No doubt many of these experimental innovations will ultimately prove to be unsuccessful, but the fact that such experimentation is still ongoing is (to me, at least) a part of what makes the Plum Blossom system so fascinating.

Appendix I

Setting up a Daily I Ching Practice

All of the greatest Chinese thinkers whose writings on the I Ching have stood the test of time have agreed on one fundamental point, often in spite of other significant differences in their perspectives: all were in accord (and usually contrary to the majority view in their intellectual culture) that the I Ching could not be understood merely by reading it alone. So naturally, the basic meaning of this is that one should actually use the I Ching for divination. But if the point is also to use the I Ching as a guide to a deeper spiritual practice (as part of one's philosophy or as part of one's "Great Work" of transformation) it is also not enough to only read the I Ching, nor even to read it and only occasionally use it in divination. The best way to incorporate the I Ching into a serious spiritual practice is to actually make a regular spiritual practice of it!

So let us first assume that you have done the basics: read the I Ching text, read as much of this book as you want to for your current level, and begun to use the I Ching for divination. Inevitably, you will want to re-examine the book at regular intervals (perhaps every six months or so), since as a "living book" the I Ching will reveal new things to you to the degree that you have been actively working with it. Likewise as your studies and understanding grows, some of the additional material in this book may become more comprehensible than it would have been at the very first reading. Studying in this way is an ongoing process.

Outside of these basics, it is also essential to have a schedule of daily practice with the I Ching (if your goal is to reach the most profound levels of understanding with it). For this, there are two steps that I think are vital. But before elaborating on these, it is necessary to point out (a little controversially) something that is not always realized: it is not vital to do an I Ching casting every day.

This is a position contrary to what many might think of as accepted wisdom or common sense; many I Ching teachers would suggest that the best way to work with the I Ching would be to cast a hexagram every single day. However, doing so can become a problematic practice. One risk with I Ching practice is that one might end up diluting it: if you are casting hexagrams constantly, this can become a source of confusion or distraction rather than a practice that creates clarity. You might "cheapen" the I Ching into something too ordinary, that ends up preventing you from making an I Ching casting into a spiritually significant event, into something that moves you out of "normal space" and into a heightened space or state of consciousness. The I Ching itself contains warning in its text about over-consultation (witness hexagram #4 for the most obvious example of this sort of warning). Doing a vague general casting each day will lead to the attitude of trying to look for things to fit that casting in the course of your day; it also creates a perspective of muddling the vastness of the I Ching. Experiencing this, some people will react to this muddle by disconnecting from the I Ching altogether, and being unable to find the insight of the castings. Others might end up becoming over-dependent on the I Ching, clinging to the notion of finding significance in the castings for every little act that takes place (note that on some level this may be viable, but on a practical level, it is usually counter-productive; unless one is a "Buddha" or a "Master of the Temple" it is impossible to actually process this degree of significance in all phenomena; and if one is at those levels, the I Ching will not be necessary to find such significance in everyday events and decisions). The over-use of castings can also lead to a situation where it is the "persona" (the Inferior Person) that dominates interpretation; where you will end up using the I Ching to tell you what your "ego" wants to hear. Ultimately, the sense of uselessness this finally creates may lead a practitioner to dismiss the utility of the I Ching altogether, blaming the tools for the failure to use them properly and "throwing out the baby with the bathwater".

But this is in no way to say that one should not be regularly engaging in castings (on an as-needed basis); nor does it mean that the I Ching is limited in the sense of only being meant for some pat definition of "exalted" or "spiritual" questions. There's no "taboo" subject in the I Ching, as long as it is a subject that is actually of significance to you.

In other words, you probably shouldn't be asking the I Ching "Should I go to the movies tonight", unless that is a question of real significance and importance to you. But if a subject does matter to you, then ask about it! The I Ching is not something that should "only" be used for abstract metaphysical ruminations, nor is it limited to only strictly material or worldly concerns. It includes "everything under heaven"; so you can ask it about your spiritual progress and the nature of reality, or you can ask it about your investments, work, romance, vacations, family, or any other mundane or personal questions. The real key is that one should cast the I Ching when there is any situation actually worthy of casting about, regardless what the subject of that question may be. This may mean that at certain times, one might in fact be casting the I Ching on a daily basis (whether to address an ongoing and developing matter, or a variety of unconnected subjects that have all come up at the same time); while at other times, one might only cast the I Ching for divination once every few weeks.

So if the actual "practice" of the I Ching does not oblige one to actually cast it for divination every day, what should constitute a daily practice?

The first and foremost answer is the contemplation of the Hexagrams themselves. There are several ways to handle this, and the goal is to familiarize one's self as much as possible with the hexagrams, and to do this in such a way that one not only studies the text but also seeks to understand the concepts and underlying significance. And it is here, and not in casting itself, where one can select a hexagram per day and allow it to permeate one's thoughts, and to look for it (and for its component trigrams) in the nature of our daily surroundings.

The secondary answer is in keeping a record. Those readers who are involved in the practice of magick will already be familiar with the "magical diary", where a practitioner keeps a daily record of his activities, practices, rituals, any insights, results, mitigating circumstances (eg., physical health, emotional state, amount of sleep, etc.) and general developments. The importance of keeping a diary is paramount: it is often the most significant determining factor between success or failure in one's progress. If you can keep a record of your I Ching studies, and of I Ching castings (how they turned out in terms of your forecasts, and what you have learned from this), and then have the ability to review all of these records months down the road, then you will grow and gain immensely in your practice. It will allow you to be reminded of what you had forgotten, and notice how your processes have changed and evolved.

It cannot be emphasized strongly enough: among those who try to engage in daily practice, the most important difference between success or failure is whether or not you KEEP A DIARY.

The diary could be a notebook, or an electronic record (but take care not to lose it, make a backup); and you should record in it every day. This creates a positive feedback-loop: writing in the diary will encourage you to actually do the practice. Make a point of opening your diary every day even if only to write "nothing to report today"; but usually, if you bother to open it at all, you'll decide to have something to report after all. It also strengthens the hexagram study itself: it makes a huge difference to actually have to copy information down, to draw the hexagram in a notebook, to write down your thoughts and discoveries about it, than to just think about these things in your head. Writing it down makes it more your own thing, it internalizes and crystallizes the experience.

The following provides a guideline for a set of daily I Ching exercises:

0. Keep a diary, record in it daily. It is better to write your insights as quickly as possible; since insights, much like dreams, tend to slip away from your memory very quickly after they occur.

1. Select a single hexagram to act as your subject for study for that day; it is probably best to go through the hexagrams in the order of the textual (King Wen) sequence, but one could theoretically choose a hexagram at random or by some other method.

2. Begin your study by reading the whole section for that hexagram, and contemplate the significance of the image, governing lines, main text, commentary, advice for the Superior Individual, and line meanings.

3. Once you have studied the text, pay attention to the hexagram itself. Look at the pairing of lines: the first and fourth, the second and fifth, the third and sixth. Do these complement each other (a broken line matching with a solid line)? Are the solid lines in their ideal positions (in lines 1, 3, or 5) and the broken lines in theirs (in lines 2, 4, and 6)?

4. The King Wen sequence, the order in which the hexagrams are arranged in the I Ching text, is based on sets of pairs; so look at each hexagram with its pair (1 with 2, 3 with 4, 5 with 6, etc., all the way to 61 with 62, and 63 with 64). Consider your hexagram of the day with relation to its paired hexagram: what is the message of these two in combination?

5. Examine the changes of each line; see which hexagram results when you change line 1 of the hexagram, then if you change line 2, then line 3, and so on. This process of changing one line and seeing what results is a key way of understanding hidden mysteries in each line; and it creates a "tree" of hexagrams related to the one you are studying. Ask yourself what the relationship is between the way that one line is described in the text, and the way the new hexagram it would form is described in the text?

6. Examine the nuclear hexagram; consider the ways in which the present hexagram is an unfolding of that nuclear hexagram. Consider the various other permutations as well: the reversed, opposite and overturned hexagrams.

Depending on the amount of time you have at your disposal, you may wish to cover all of these points each day; or you may wish to do only one point at a time each day, or do a single point for sixty-four days, then proceed to the next point in succession until you have eventually done each of the different points of I Ching study in a gradual and progressive fashion.

It is strongly recommended that you take notes of all your studies in your diary; in fact, the first time you go through the core material (point 2 above) you should copy out the hexagram image, and the core text and lines at least in point form, if not in full. This might seem like pointless busy-work at first glance; after all, you own this book, so why would you need to copy the material into a notebook?! However, there is a powerful effect on the brain in copying out information with your own hand; it goes beyond just reading, it rewires neural pathways at a level that does not happen by merely glancing at the text. As you draw the hexagram, as you write out its meanings, those images and meanings become your own within your consciousness.

This course of study is in addition to any castings you may perform, which should also be meticulously recorded.

All of this work is not easy; but the rewards are great. If you engage with the I Ching on a daily basis, you will soon discover levels of understanding that were not previously apparent. This will result in shifts of consciousness in your everyday life: you will begin to look at your surroundings differently, at your relationships differently, and at the nature of time and change in different ways. You will find that through such study, the ease and depth of your divination castings will increase remarkably. The key is not in studying intensely, but in studying consistently. If you go through working with the I Ching in fits and starts (going long periods without referencing the work) then the opportunity for progress is more limited, even if when you do study it you are doing a great amount of work. In my own experience, it is much better to spend even ten or fifteen minutes on the I Ching every day than to study the I Ching for five hours one day, and then not at all for the next three. The practice progresses through consistency and regular discipline (as the I Ching itself so often advocates); so if there are days when you find yourself so harried that you cannot do the whole of the study you had set out to do, it is still better at the very least to give the I Ching some very minor, very short consideration, than to do nothing at all. And as with any discipline, you will find that the more regularly you practice it, the easier it will become to practice regularly.

Appendix II

Aleister Crowley and the I Ching

It would not be exaggeration to state that Aleister Crowley (1875-1947) was the most influential figure in western occultism of the twentieth century. He revolutionized ideas in ceremonial magick, incorporated raja-yoga and other Indian teachings into western occultism in new and exciting ways (that were more authentic to the spirit of the original sources than previous attempts), founded the religion of Thelema, was directly influential on the founder of Wicca (to the point that much of Crowley's ritual writing was cut-and-pasted into the original Gardnerian "Book of Shadows"), and became a counter-culture icon of the 1960s that significantly influenced art, music, and film (and continues to do so).

This appendix will not attempt to present his biography (there are many other sources which can be found with a cursory search that do this job admirably). Instead, it is meant to focus on one specific aspect of Crowley's life and work that was likewise tremendously revolutionary in the West: Crowley's relationship to the I Ching.

Aleister Crowley was not the first westerner to have an encounter with the I Ching; it had, after all, been known to westerners since the seventeenth century at least, and Jesuit missionary priests had translated the text. What makes Crowley remarkable was his approach to the I Ching (which was novel), and the way he related the I Ching to his magical and Thelemic system.

It isn't absolutely certain when Crowley first became aware of the I Ching; there's some possibility that his very first exposure to the I Ching may have taken place in 1900, when Crowley was visiting San Francisco. He may have seen the I Ching in practice in that city's sizable Chinatown (which would have contained various sensual delights of interest to him). However, this is unverified. What is certain is that Crowley had definitely experienced the I Ching by 1905, when he engaged in a lengthy trip across parts of China. His diary records that by the time he had reached Shanghai, his curiosity regarding the I Ching led him to commence what would become a growing focus of his study for the remaining four decades of his life.

It is equally evident that while Crowley might have seen the I Ching in use (be it in San Francisco or in China itself), he did not manage to find anyone capable of instructing him personally in the traditional methods of its use. We know this because Crowley never, in all his voluminous public and private writings, gave any evidence of being familiar with any of the traditional methods of I Ching casting (be it with coins, yarrow stalks, or methods like the Plum Blossom system). Nor could Crowley have learned this method by his own untutored research; he could not read Chinese, and the only source of the I Ching text available to him was James Legge's 1882 translation (published as part of the "Sacred Books of the East" series). Legge's work was academic, very imperfect by modern standards, and significantly Victorian in its outlook. Crowley himself was aware of the limitations of this edition (and in his typical fashion criticized the quality of Legge's often-ponderous writing by giving him the nickname of "Wooden Legge"), but no alternative was available to him. Crucially, in this original edition of Legge's work, no instructions were provided as to how to actually perform an I Ching casting (note that later printings of Legge's translation do often have such instructions added in). As a Victorian academic and a devout Christian, Legge no doubt felt that such information was not actually significant to the value of the I Ching as an historical text. In the English-speaking world, accurate instructions on the I Ching's use in divination would not become readily available until the Wilhelm edition was translated into English, several years after Crowley's death.

Thus, without any clear guide as to how to actually perform I Ching divination in any traditional fashion, Crowley was obliged to develop his own method. Possibly inspired by the witnessing of Chinese divination sticks, Crowley's way of consulting the I Ching involved the use of six sticks, with a Yang (solid) line on one side and a Yin (broken) line on the other, laid out in order, to create a randomly generated hexagram. While there's some indication that Crowley was familiar with the use of changing lines, his diaries indicate that he did not generally make use of these; instead, in his castings he would read the main text and then read all six lines, in order. He would then try to use all six lines of his single hexagram to generate some kind of narrative about the situation at hand.

In spite of these limitations, the more remarkable detail in this story is that Crowley was the first westerner we know of to regularly rely on the I Ching for divination purposes. And the evidence of Crowley's diaries reveals that, despite having been forced to rely on a method of his own devising, a method that certainly failed in many respects to take full advantage of the advantages of the I Ching in terms of its full potential to measure time and space, his system was still sound enough to work sufficiently well for Crowley to rely on it in his daily life for both spiritual and practical purposes. In general, his use of the I Ching for divination increased over the course of his life. While Crowley was familiar with a variety of systems of western divination, including the Tarot, Geomancy, and Astrology, there is no doubt from the evidence that the I Ching was by far his favourite for regular and practical use. At several points in his life, his diaries note the details of several I Ching divinations per day.

Crowley wrote his own (very abbreviated and largely unorthodox) poetic re-interpretation of the I Ching; and while he never published a book on the I Ching in his lifetime, in the final decade of his life Crowley was engaged in collecting his notes on the I Ching, possibly in preparation for a writing project that would have followed the ambitious "Book of Thoth" and "Thoth Tarot" project he'd undertaken with Lady Frieda Harris.

While the limitations of Crowley's education on the I Ching was often quite evident (and has been a regular source of criticism against him by academics), considering the poor sources of information available to him in his lifetime, this is perhaps less astounding than the quality of some of his insights into the I Ching which could only have been the product of his own insight.

For example, there are notable similarities in Crowley's approach to the I Ching in his writings to the teachings of the ancient "Image and Number" school of I Ching thought, in spite of the fact that Crowley had almost certainly never heard of this school. On a similar note, Crowley's choice of description for the trigrams (one part of Crowley's system that has influenced the trigram descriptions used in this book) were selected as part of his attempt to synthesize the concepts he found in the I Ching to his western symbolic language; and yet at the same time (again, potentially unbeknownst to Crowley) these attributions were not "foreign" or "mislabelled" as some critics claim, but rather all fit into attributions that Chinese scholars themselves have given to the trigrams over the centuries.

In general, it is evident that awareness and states of enhanced consciousness brought about by Crowley's highly disciplined spiritual practices (in western magick and Indian yoga/meditation), as well as consistent and serious practice in the I Ching itself, proved their worth in granting Crowley particular insights into aspects of the I Ching he could not have merely studied through intellectual research. It is equally evident, and equally fascinating, that this "enlightened perspective" did not allow him to have uniformly "authentic" understandings. Rather, Crowley was at his best with regard to the I Ching in his observations of the deepest or most sublime aspects of the I Ching cosmology: the Tao, Yin and Yang, and the Trigrams. That is, those parts of the I Ching that emerge most directly from the study of the nature of reality itself. He was far less remarkable in his insights on the hexagrams, the text of the I Ching and theories about interpretation of meanings, and divination methods. That is, with those parts that did not emerge purely from the study of reality but were partly the "work of man".

Of equal interest was Crowley's effort to correlate the I Ching to the system of western magick. It was his life-long goal to create a grand unified structure of occult symbolism, to fulfil the promise of the Qabalah in uncovering the underlying language, the "perennial philosophy" spoken of since at least the time of Pythagoras that explained the threads and connections between all symbolic systems in esoteric teaching. Many of the correspondences detailed within this book are based on the insights Crowley developed over time in connecting the I Ching symbols to the western esoteric road-map. Having chosen to identify the trigram by titles and concepts that best fit the western framework, he proceeded to map the I Ching hexagrams onto the Tree of Life of the Qabalah. It is noteworthy here that over time Crowley's understanding of these correspondences evolved; his attributions early on in his I Ching studies (when he published "777", an encyclopedia of the Qabalah) were different than his final attributions published almost four decades later (in "the Book of Thoth", his masterpiece on the Tarot). Sadly, his work on this important task was never completed, but he presented enough to provide important groundwork on the understanding of the I Ching's correspondences to western thought.

The fact that Crowley's views on these subjects evolved over time demonstrates that like any serious student of the I Ching, he did not rest on his first assumptions about the system, but rather continued to refine his studies as his practical experience with divination and the text of the I Ching advanced. This is important because we can speculate that had Crowley been presented with the opportunity to revise his understandings with more efficient translations, more complete texts, or access to some of the writings of the various historical I Ching scholars, he would not likely have stood pat on his theories, or his divination methods as he practised them. Thelemites and other admirers of Crowley would thus be doing him a disservice by simply slavishly imitating Crowley's divination technique, or resting their understanding of the I Ching solely on Crowley's operating ideas. The only viable conclusion with regards to approaching Crowley's contribution to the western I Ching today is to carefully examine what he wrote and practised, retain from these things that which proves useful in the larger context of I Ching studies, and modify or leave behind those parts that ought to be adjusted in the light of greater access to information about the rich three-thousand year history of I Ching teachings now accessible.

Appendix III

Reference Tables

A: Hexagram Table

Top Trigram → / Bottom Trigram	Heaven	World	Sun	Moon	Fire	Water	Air	Earth
Heaven	1	11	14	5	34	43	9	26
World	12	2	35	8	16	45	20	23
Sun	13	36	30	63	55	49	37	22
Moon	6	7	64	29	40	47	59	4
Fire	25	24	21	3	51	17	42	27
Water	10	19	38	60	54	58	61	41
Air	44	46	50	48	32	28	57	18
Earth	33	15	56	39	62	31	53	52

B: The Trigrams

☰ "Chien": Heaven

Chien is the trigram traditionally translated as "Heaven". It is pure Yang, solid and unbroken. It is the celestial power, all the energy of creating, strong, the cold force, the masculine, the phallus, light, the father. It is the quality of forcefulness. Its key spiritual concept is "Creative".

☷ "Kun": The World

Kun is the trigram traditionally translated as "earth", but its meaning is "The World" (the opposite of Chien, which is "Heaven"). Kun is pure Yin, broken lines. It is the worldly power, all the content of creation, weak, the hot force, the feminine, the yoni, darkness, the mother. It is the quality of spaciousness; as Heaven is the "force", so is World the "field". Its key spiritual concept is "Receptive".

☲ "Li": The Sun

Li has traditionally been translated as "fire", but this is the concept of pure primordial fire, not the lesser elemental fire. Thus, the best translation for this trigram is another historical attribution, which would put it in line with what "Li" is meant to represent in western esotericism: "The Sun". It is sometimes also referred to as "lightning". It is the trigram associated with summer (when the sun is at its strongest), beauty, the power of clinging. Because it is a single weak line between two strong ones, it is referred to as the "middle daughter". Its quality is radiance. Its key spiritual concept is "Elegance".

☵ "Kan": The Moon

Kan has been traditionally translated as "water", but in the same way that Li represents primordial fire, Kan represents primordial water, thus another traditional attribution is a more appropriate one for western correspondence: "The Moon". It is also referred to sometimes as the cloud, or the pit. It can represent "danger", because of its hidden power (a strong line surrounded by weak lines). It is associated with winter (when the sun is at its weakest), the characteristic of enveloping; and because of the strong line in the middle it is called the "middle son". Its quality is depth. Its key spiritual concept is "Abysmal" (i.e., "Deep").

☳ "Chen": The Fire Element

The trigram "Chen" is traditionally translated as "thunder", but its quality is that of the hermetic element of Fire. It is the active and moving force, the force of dynamic power, the arousing or energetic force. It is correspondent to springtime, the time of rising force. Because of its single strong line at the bottom (the first line of the trigram, because in the I Ching the lines are always read from the bottom to the top), it is called the "eldest son". Its quality is vibration. Its key spiritual concept is "Arousing" (i.e., "Exciting").

☱ "Tui": The Water Element

The trigram "Tui" is traditionally translated as "lake", but its quality is that of the hermetic element of Water. It is the deep and still force. It corresponds to autumn, when nature is slowing down. It is also sometimes translated as "a marsh", or even a "swamp" (but this is somewhat inaccurate, as it is not meant to have any of the negative connotations westerners associate with swamps). It has the quality of the rain, of joy and relaxed pleasure. Because of its broken line at the top, it is called the "youngest daughter". Its quality is openness. Its key spiritual concept is "Pleasant" (or "Complacent").

☴ "Sun": The Air Element

The trigram "Sun" is traditionally translated as "wind", but its quality is that of the hermetic element of Air, which is also part of its traditional attributions. It is sometimes also translated as "wood", which is correspondent in Taoist alchemy to some of the concepts of the Air element, and like the hermetic air element corresponds to the intellect. It has a gentle quality, but insistent. Because of its weak line at the bottom, it is called the "eldest daughter". Its quality is consideration. Its key spiritual concept is "Flexible".

☶ "Ken": The Earth Element

The trigram "Ken" is traditionally translated as "mountain", but its quality is that of the hermetic element of Earth, which attribution is clearly included in its traditional symbolism. It is the immovable solid power, and has the quality of stubbornness and stuckness. Because of its strong line at the top, it is called the "youngest son". Its quality is attachment. Its key spiritual concept is "Solid".

C: A Quick Look-up of Nuclear Hexagrams

Hexagram #:	Is a Nuclear Hexagram of:
1	28, 43, 44
2	23, 24 27
63	38, 40, 54
64	37, 39, 53

The following hexagrams are all nuclear hexagrams of #1, 2, 63 or 64, and are in turn nuclear hexagrams of:

Hexagram # (nuclear):		Is a Nuclear Hexagram of:
23	(2)	3, 8, 20, 42
24	(2)	4, 7, 19, 41
27	(2)	29, 59, 60, 61
28	(1)	30, 55, 56, 62
37	(64)	6, 10, 47, 58
38	(63)	5, 9, 48, 57
39	(64)	16, 21, 35, 51
40	(63)	15, 22, 36, 52
43	(1)	14, 32, 34, 50
44	(1)	13, 31, 33, 49
53	(64)	12, 17, 25, 45
54	(63)	11, 18, 26, 46

D: Plum Blossom Method:

Summary of Plum Blossom Method Standard Procedure

1. Calculate number values for date, time, month, and year, converted from the Chinese Lunar Calendar.

2. Calculate lower trigram of main hexagram by adding values for:

Hour + Day + Month + Year

then divide by eight and use the remainder to determine the trigram.

3. Calculate upper trigram of main hexagram by adding values for:

Day + Month + Year

then divide by eight and use the remainder to determine the trigram.

4. Calculate the changing line of the hexagram by adding the values for:

Hour + Day + Month + Year

then divide by six, and the remainder is the line that is changing (a result with no remainder means line 6 is the changing line).

5. Generate the Future hexagram in the standard fashion.

6. Generate the Nuclear hexagram in the standard fashion.

7. Study the image of the hexagram, as well as the main text description, and the changing line oracle.

8. Study the images and main texts of the Nuclear Hexagram and the Future Hexagram. Contemplate all of the above carefully.

9. In the main hexagram, the "Subject" trigram is the trigram that does not contain a changing line. Compare this trigram to each other trigram in turn on the list of elemental compatibilities; beginning with the other main hexagram trigram to determine the overall current situation, then with the lower and upper nuclear trigrams to determine the other influences upon the situation, and finally the two trigrams of the future hexagram to determine future developments of the situation.

Number Value for Hours of the Day

Western Hour:	Hour Value:
11pm–1am	1
1am–3am	2
3am–5am	3
5am–7am	4
7am–9am	5
9am–11am	6
11am–1pm	7
1pm–3pm	8
3pm–5pm	9
5pm–7pm	10
7pm–9pm	11
9pm–11pm	12

Number Value for Year

Chinese Zodiac Year:	Number Value:
Rat	1
Ox	2
Tiger	3
Rabbit/Hare	4
Dragon	5
Snake	6
Horse	7
Goat/Sheep	8
Monkey	9
Rooster	10

Dog	11
Boar/Pig	12

Lunar Calendar Conversions found:

http://www.hko.gov.hk/gts/time/conversion1_text.htm

Hexagram Remainder Numbers

Remainder	*Trigram*
1	Heaven
2	Water
3	Sun
4	Fire
5	Air
6	Moon
7	Earth
8 (0)	World

Plum Blossom Trigram Comparison Table: Fate Trigram

Subject	Fire	Air	Sun	Earth	World	Heaven	Water	Moon
Fire	S	S	R	C	C	E	E	G
Air	S	S	R	C	C	E	E	G
Sun	G	G	S	R	R	C	C	E
Earth	E	E	G	S	S	R	R	C
World	E	E	G	S	S	R	R	C
Heaven	C	C	E	G	G	S	S	R
Water	C	C	E	G	G	S	S	R
Moon	C	C	E	G	G	S	S	R

Explanation of Codes

S: These fate trigrams strengthen the subject. The situation is positive and easy at this stage; the subject and the situation are in mutual accord.

R: These fate trigrams reduce the subject. The situation is inauspicious, and only considerable effort, discipline, and hard work can prevail here. The subject has the potential to be in command over the situation.

C: These fate trigrams clash with the subject. The situation is tumultuous, but this too can be auspicious. It is important to be very careful, because it is easy for fortune to be disrupted. It is necessary to move carefully, and take advantage of change without bringing on unnecessary conflict or opposition. The subject must take command of the situation.

E: These fate trigrams eliminate the subject. The situation is highly inauspicious at this stage. It is only mitigated by judicious application of virtue, and careful conservative choices. The situation overwhelms the subject; it is beyond the subject's control.

G: These fate trigrams generate the subject. The situation has the potential to be very auspicious, if the subject is willing to move along with it. The situation is beyond the subject's control; but if the subject accords to the reality of the situation, the result is positive.

References

Balkin, J. (2002). *The Laws of Change: I Ching and the Philosophy of Life*. New York: Schocken.

Blofeld, J. (1965). *I Ching, The Book of Change*. New York: Dutton.

Ching, J. (2000). *The Religious Thought of Chu Hsi*. New York: Oxford.

Crowley, A. (1986). *777 and Other Qabalistic Writings of Aleister Crowley*. New York: Weiser.

Ibid. (1972). *The Book of Changes*. San Francisco, CA: Level.

Ibid. (1974). *The Book of Thoth*. York Beach, ME: Weiser.

Ibid. (2004). *Liber AL vel Legis: The Book of the Law (centennial edition)*. New York: Weiser.

Ibid., & Skinner, S. (Ed). (1996). *The Magical Diaries of Aleister Crowley: Tunisia 1923 (subsequent edition)*. New York: Weiser.

Fancourt, W. & Moore, S. (Ed.). (1995-2000). *The Oracle: The Journal of Yijing Studies* (11 vol.).

Huang, A. (2000). *The Numerology of the I Ching: A Sourcebook of Symbols, Structures, and Traditional Wisdom*. Rochester, NY: Inner Traditions.

Hulse, D. (1993). *The Key of It All*. St. Paul, MN: Llewellyn.

Kaczynski, R. (2010). *Perdurabo: The Life of Aleister Crowley (revised and expanded edition)*. Berkeley, CA: North Atlantic.

Legge, J. (1963). *The I Ching*. New York: Dover.

Liu, D. (1975). *I Ching Numerology*. San Francisco, CA: Harper.

Lynn, R. (1994). *The Classic of Changes*. New York: Columbia.

McKenna, D. & McKenna, T. (1994). *The Invisible Landscape: Mind, Hallucinogens, and the I Ching (Reprint Edition)*. San Francisco, CA: Harper.

Schoter, A. (2005). The Yijing as a Symbolic Language for Abstraction. *Proceedings of the 2nd International Conference on I-Ching (Yijing) Studies and Contemporary Civilization*: 291-305. International Association of I Ching Studies: Yongkang City, Taiwan.

Shaughnessy, E. (1996). *I Ching: The Classic of Changes*. New York: Ballantine.

Sherrill, W. & Chu, W. (1989). *An Anthology of I Ching*. London: Arkana.

Smith, K., Bol, P., Adler, J., & Wyatt, D. (1990). *Sung Dynasty Uses of the I Ching*. Princeton, NJ: Princeton University Press.

Wilhelm, R. & Baynes, C., (Trans). (1967). *The I Ching or Book of Changes*. Princeton, NJ: Princeton University Press.

Websites

Lunar Calendar Conversion Charts. Hong Kong Observatory.
  http://www.hko.gov.hk/gts/time/conversion1_text.htm

Yijing Dao.
  http://www.biroco.com/yijing/index.htm

Yijing.
  http://www.yijing.co.uk/index.html

To continue your I Ching studies, please join us at "The Magician's I Ching" facebook group:

https://www.facebook.com/groups/346543022152305/

For more instruction on universal mysticism in general, please visit the author's YouTube channel and website:

https://www.youtube.com/user/SwamijiNisarg/videos

http://www.mystery-school.net/